ENVIRONMENTAL STUDIES

LOOKING AROUND

TEXTBOOK FOR CLASS IV

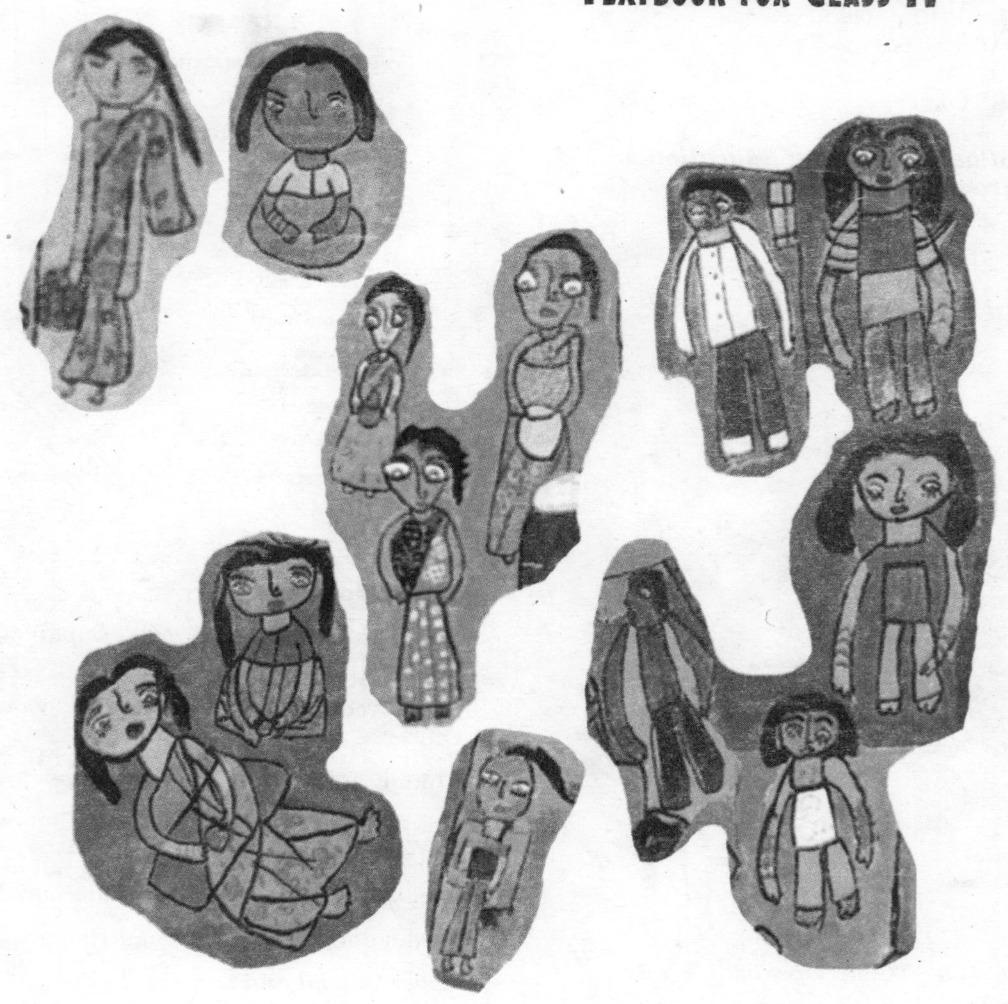

राष्ट्रीय शैक्षिक अनुसंधान और प्रशिक्षण परिषद्
NATIONAL COUNCIL OF EDUCATIONAL RESEARCH AND TRAINING

ISBN 81-7450-664-0

First Edition
February 2007 Magha 1928

Reprinted
November 2007 Kartika 1929
February 2009 Phalguna 1930
January 2010 Magha 1931
March 2011 Phalguna 1932
January 2012 Magha 1933
March 2013 Phalguna 1934
October 2013 Asvina 1935
December 2014 Pausa 1936

PD 465T IJ

₹ 50.00

Cover Artwork
Tahera Pathan and Rabia Sheikh
Himmat, Ahmedabad

Printed on 80 GSM paper with NCERT watermark

Published at the Publication Division by the Secretary, National Council of Educational Research and Training, Sri Aurobindo Marg, New Delhi 110 016 and printed at Shagun Offset Pvt. Ltd., B-3, Sector-65, Noida 201 301 (UP)

OFFICES OF THE PUBLICATION DIVISION, NCERT

NCERT Campus
Sri Aurobindo Marg
New Delhi 110 016 — **Phone : 011-26562708**

108, 100 Feet Road
Hosdakere Halli Extension
Banashankari III Stage
Bangalore 560 085 — **Phone : 080-26725740**

Navjivan Trust Building
P.O.Navjivan
Ahmedabad 380 014 — **Phone : 079-27541446**

CWC Campus
Opp. Dhankal Bus Stop
Panihati
Kolkata 700 114 — **Phone : 033-25530454**

CWC Complex
Maligaon
Guwahati 781 021 — **Phone : 0361-2674869**

Publication Team

Head, Publication Division	:	*N. K. Gupta*
Chief Production Officer	:	*Kalyan Banerjee*
Chief Editor	:	*Shveta Uppal*
Chief Business Manager	:	*Gautam Ganguly*
Assistant Editor	:	*Hemant Kumar*
Production Assistant	:	*Sunil Kumar*

Cover Design and Layout
Shweta Rao

Illustrations
Joel Gill, Alok Hari, Arup Gupta, Manish Raj, Deepa Balsavar, Centre for Environment Education and Avehi Abacus Project

FOREWORD

The National Curriculum Framework (NCF) 2005, recommends that children's life at school must be linked to their life outside the school. This principle marks a departure from the legacy of bookish learning which continues to shape our system and causes a gap between the school, home and community. The syllabi and textbooks developed on the basis of NCF signify an attempt to implement this basic idea. They also attempt to discourage rote learning and the maintenance of sharp boundaries between different subject areas. We hope these measures will take us significantly further in the direction of a child-centred system of education outlined in the National Policy on Education (1986).

The success of this effort depends on what steps that school principals and teachers will take to encourage children to reflect on their own learning and to pursue imaginative activities and questions. We must recognise that, given space, time and freedom, children generate new knowledge by engaging with the information passed on to them by adults. Treating the prescribed textbook as the sole basis of examination is one of the key reasons why other resources and sites of learning are ignored. Inculcating creativity and initiative is possible if we perceive and treat children as participants in learning, not as receivers of a fixed body of knowledge.

These aims imply considerable change in school routines and mode of functioning. Flexibility in the daily time-table is as necessary as rigour in implementing the annual calendar so that the required number of teaching days are actually devoted to teaching. The methods used for teaching and evaluation will also determine how effective this textbook proves for making children's life at school a happy experience, rather than a source of stress or boredom. Syllabus designers have tried to address the problem of curricular burden by restructuring and reorienting knowledge at different stages with greater consideration for child psychology and the time available for teaching. The textbook attempts to enhance this endeavour by giving higher priority and space to opportunities for contemplation and wondering, discussion in small groups, and activities requiring hands-on experience.

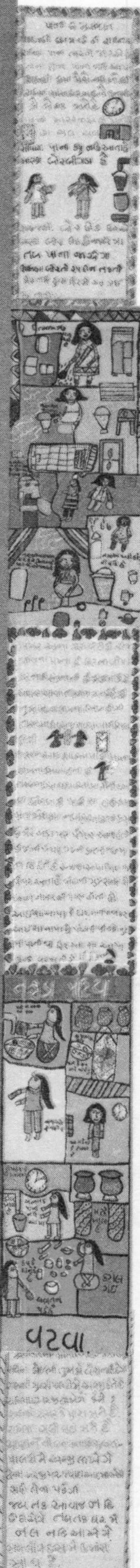

The National Council of Educational Research and Training (NCERT) appreciates the hard work done by the textbook development committee responsible for this book. We wish to thank the Chairperson of the Advisory Committee for Textbooks at the the primary level, Anita Rampal, *Professor*, CIE, Delhi University, Delhi, Chief Advisor, Savithri Singh, *Principal,* Acharya Narendra Dev College, University of Delhi, New Delhi, Co-chief Advisor, Farah Farooqi, *Reader*, Jamia Millia Islamia, Delhi, for guiding the work of this committee. Several teachers contributed to the development of this

textbook. We are grateful to their principals for making this possible. We are indebted to the institutions and organisations which have generously permitted us to draw upon their resources, material and personnel. We are especially grateful to the members of the National Monitoring Committee, appointed by the Department of Secondary and Higher Education, Ministry of Human Resource Development under the Chairpersonship of Professor Mrinal Miri and Professor G.P. Deshpande, for their valuable time and contribution.

As an organisation committed to systemic reform and continuous improvement in the quality of its products, NCERT welcomes comments and suggestions which will enable us to undertake further revision and refinement.

Director
National Council of Educational
Research and Training

New Delhi
20 November 2006

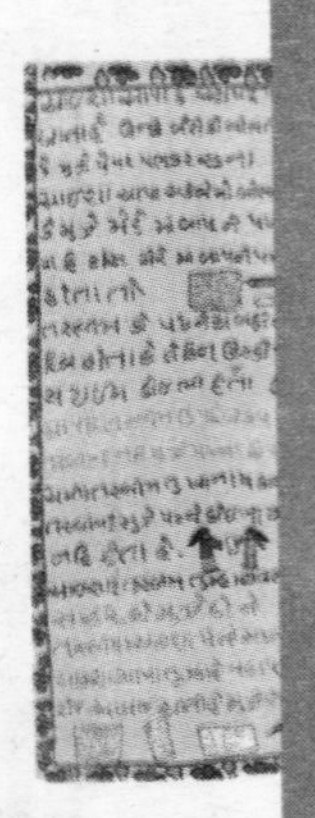

A Note for the Teachers and Parents

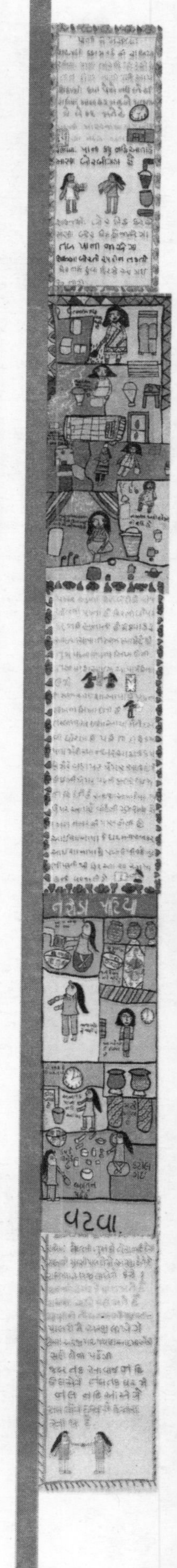

The team for the development of this book found it a challenging task to translate the objectives as defined in the National Curriculum Framework (NCF) 2005 while preparing this national-level textbook. The writing team would like to share some of the issues that were discussed during the process.

The child looks at the environment around her/him in a holistic manner and does not compartmentalise any topic into 'science' and 'social science', hence, it was thought essential that we too aim for this integration within the book, instead of having two disparate sections. Instead of proceeding with lists of 'topics', the syllabus itself has proposed themes that allowed a connected and inter-related understanding to develop. An attempt has been made in the book to locate every theme in physical, social and cultural contexts critically so that the child can make informed choices.

The challenge, when writing at a national-level, was to reflect the multicultural dimensions of diverse classrooms. It was felt necessary that all children feel important – their community, culture, and their way of life – are all important. While writing the book – *Who is the child we are addressing* – was the big question. Is she/he the child in big schools of the metro, or the school in the slums, a small-town child, one in a village *shala* or the one in the remote mountainous area? How do we address such diverse group? One also needed to tackle the differences of gender, class, culture, religion, language, geographical location, etc. These are some of the issues addressed in the book, which the teacher will also have to handle in her own ways.

The content in the book is centred on the child, providing her/him a lot of space to explore. There is a conscious effort to discourage rote learning and hence descriptions and definitions were totally avoided. It is always easy to give information; the real challenge was to provide opportunities to a child where she/he can vocalise, build upon her/his curiosity, learn-by-doing, ask questions, experiment, etc. In order that the child is happy to engage with the book, a variety of formats have been used – narratives, poems, stories, puzzles, jigsaw, comic strips, etc. Stories and narratives have been used as a tool for sensitising the child since a child can probably more easily empathise with characters in a story or a narrative. The language used in the book is not formal but is in the 'commonly spoken' form.

Active participation of children is very important in constructing knowledge. Activities in the book that demand that children be taken for observations to the parks, fields, water-bodies, into the community, etc., reiterates that EVS learning primarily occurs outside the walls of the classrooms. An effort has been made to relate the child's local knowledge to the school knowledge. It is important to state here

that the activities given in the book are only suggestive and that both the activities and the materials can and should be, modified by the teacher according to the local contexts. Activities and exercises have been inbuilt into the chapters instead of being pushed to the end. The nature of activities in the book are so varied so that the child gets opportunities to explore, observe, draw, categorise, speak, question, write, list, etc. Several activities allow her/him to manipulate things with her/his hands so that her/his psychomotor skills are developed. Some of them explore her/his creativity and design skills as well as hone her/his aesthetic sense. All activities need to be followed by discussions to facilitate children in consolidating what they have observed and learnt. With an appropriate question or suggestion, the child's understanding can be extended far beyond the point which she/he could have reached alone.

Children are encouraged to tap sources other than the textbook and teachers, such as family members, members of the community, newspapers, story books, other reading material, etc. This stresses the fact that textbooks are not the only sources of information. To develop a sense of history, the children are encouraged to question the elderly about the past. These activities also promote the parents' and community's involvement in the school and the teacher gets an opportunity to know a child's background.

Illustrations form an important component of children's books. The writing team has kept in mind that the illustrations in this book reflect the ethos of the written material. Content development through illustrations was a major consideration. The illustrations have been used such that they complement the writing style fully. The illustrations should provide joy and also a challenge, to the child.

The book provides varied kind of opportunities for the child to work – individually, in small groups or even in larger groups. Group learning promotes peer learning and improves social interactions. Children particularly enjoy learning crafts and arts while working in groups. Children are very happy and respond with enthusiasm when their creative ventures are appreciated rather than dismissed (as unimportant).

The objective of the activities and questions in the book is not only to evaluate the child's knowledge but also to provide an opportunity to the children to express themselves. The children should be given enough time to work on these activities and questions; they should not be rushed since each child learns at her/his own pace. It is envisaged that each teacher will develop her/his own evaluation tools suitable for her/his students based on her/his own method of teaching and local contexts. The child should be evaluated primarily on the skills she/he has acquired while working in class or outside. Evaluation, of course, should be a continuous process and the child should be assessed as she/he observes, asks, draws, discusses in groups, etc.

One of the major concerns while developing textual materials was to find suitable ways to sensitise the child to the wide differences that exist within our society – in our physical abilities, economic backgrounds, behavioural patterns, etc. – things which get reflected in the way and where we live, what kind of school we go to, the way we talk, the way we think, what we eat, what we wear, our access to basic amenities, etc. We would like every child to recognise that in any society there are differences; we need to learn to appreciate and respect these differences. Teachers have to be extra-careful that such social issues are handled in a sensitive manner, especially when there are children with special needs or in difficult circumstances, in the class.

This book also brings to you some more significant elements. The bulk of the chapters in the book are based on examples from contemporary life. The chapters either tell stories of real events or inform us about exciting characters drawn from everyday life as life itself is a rich source of information and learning. Further, narratives from real life inspire us, they can bring to us an interesting point of reference, they can provide us an opportunity to revisit experiences we are familiar with.

These narrative range from success stories, achievements and also instances of disturbing behaviour patterns. The instance we selected are from the lives of lesser known people rather than from the lives of celebrities as we feel that the lives of ordinary people can be a greater inspiration and lessen the distance between object and subject. It is hoped that those exposed to these narratives will relate with them creatively rather than take them at face value. Through activities and discussion points in each chapter, great care is taken to provide such opportunities. It must be stressed that the selections are not to be viewed like an 'instant meal' to be consumed without further processing – none of the narratives, positive or negative, are intended to be blindly emulated or looked down upon and discarded. It is hoped that children and adults alike will critique them on the basis of their own unique experience, core values and skills of analysis. Such a process will enrich teaching-learning and add a dimension to children's way of understanding the book of life as they mature.

The writing team looks not only at the children, but at the teachers also, as individuals who construct knowledge and build on their own experiences. The textbook is only one of the many teaching-learning materials used by teachers. Thus, this textbook should only be viewed as an aid to the teacher, around which the teacher could organise her teaching to provide learning opportunities to children.

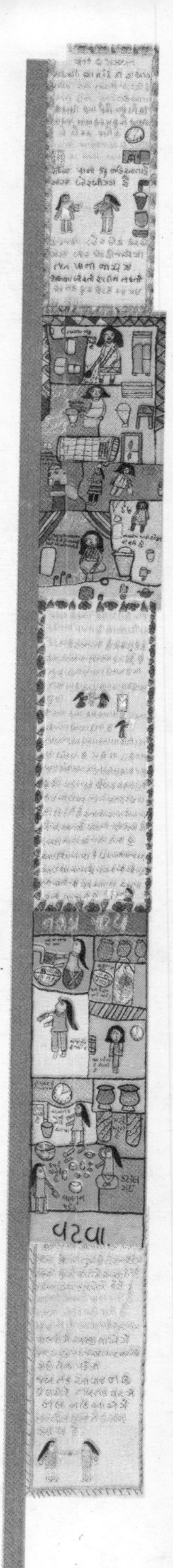

S. Amal Jerry Arputharaj, 10 years,
St. Patrick Modern Higher Secondary School, Pondicherry

Textbook Development Committee

Chairperson, Advisory Committee for Textbooks at the Primary Level

Anita Rampal, *Professor,* Department of Education (CIE), University of Delhi, Delhi

Chief Advisor

Savithri Singh, *Principal,* Acharya Narendra Dev College, University of Delhi, Delhi

Co-chief Advisor

Farah Farooqi, *Reader*, Faculty of Education, Jamia Millia Islamia, Delhi

Members

Latika Gupta, *Consultant,* SSA, DEE, NCERT, New Delhi

Mamata Pandya, *Programme Director,* Centre for Environment Education, Ahmedabad

Poonam Mongia, *Teacher,* Sarvodaya Kanya Vidyalaya, Vikas Puri, New Delhi

Reena Ahuja, *Programme Officer,* National Education Group-FIRE, Gautam Nagar, New Delhi

Sangeeta Arora, *Primary Teacher,* Kendriya Vidyalaya, Shalimar Bagh, New Delhi

Simantini Dhuru, *Director,* Avehi Abacus Project, Mumbai

Swati Verma, *Teacher,* The Heritage School, Rohini, New Delhi

Member-coordinator

Manju Jain, *Professor,* Department of Elementary Education, NCERT, New Delhi

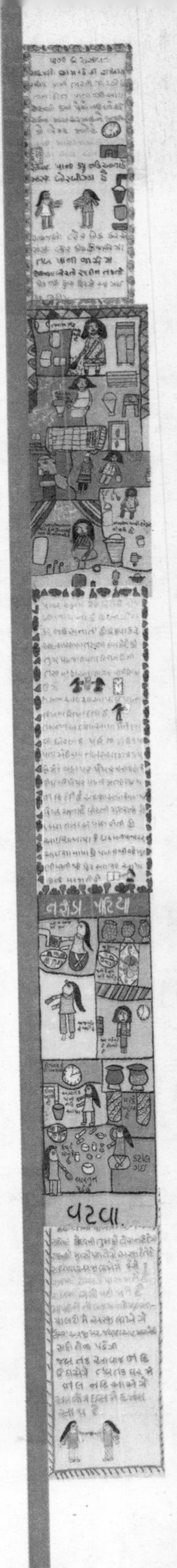

ACKNOWLEDGEMENTS

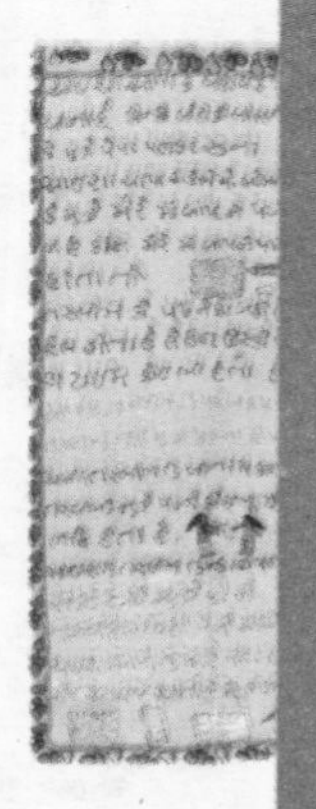

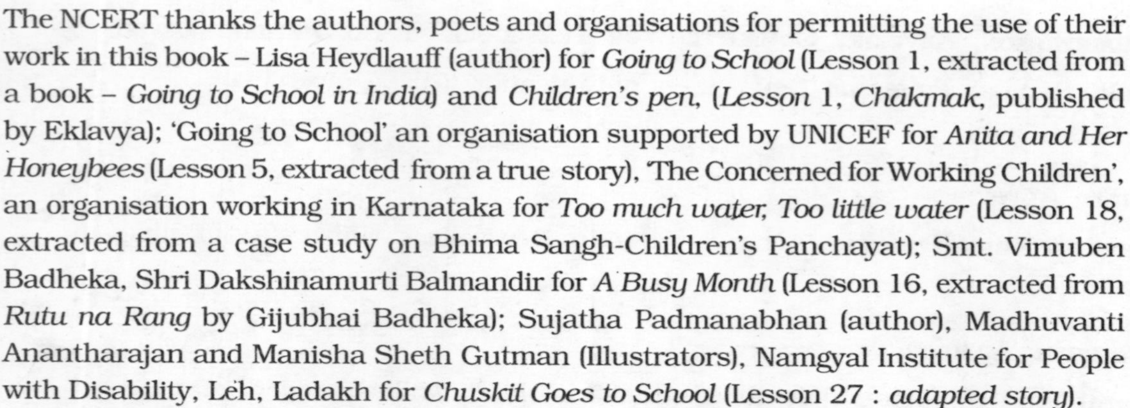
The NCERT thanks the authors, poets and organisations for permitting the use of their work in this book – Lisa Heydlauff (author) for *Going to School* (Lesson 1, extracted from a book – *Going to School in India*) and *Children's pen*, (*Lesson* 1, *Chakmak*, published by Eklavya); 'Going to School' an organisation supported by UNICEF for *Anita and Her Honeybees* (Lesson 5, extracted from a true story), 'The Concerned for Working Children', an organisation working in Karnataka for *Too much water, Too little water* (Lesson 18, extracted from a case study on Bhima Sangh-Children's Panchayat); Smt. Vimuben Badheka, Shri Dakshinamurti Balmandir for *A Busy Month* (Lesson 16, extracted from *Rutu na Rang* by Gijubhai Badheka); Sujatha Padmanabhan (author), Madhuvanti Anantharajan and Manisha Sheth Gutman (Illustrators), Namgyal Institute for People with Disability, Leh, Ladakh for *Chuskit Goes to School* (Lesson 27 : *adapted story*).

We are grateful to Shri S. Vinayak, AMO, SSA, Andhra Pradesh for collecting children's essay on Pochampalli Sarees and Ms K. Kalyani, Lady Sri Ram College, Delhi University for translating the same (Lesson 23). We express our thanks to the Centre for Environment Education, Ahmedabad and Avehi Abacus, Mumbai for use of their publications that formed the base for some of the lessons. The contribution of the following Organisations, Institutions for deputing experts is also highly appreciated – Director, Centre for Environment Education, Ahmedabad; Director, Avehi Abacus, Mumbai; Principal, Kendriya Vidyalaya, Shalimar Bagh, Delhi; Principal, Sarvodaya Kanya Vidyalaya, Vikas Puri, New Delhi; Principal, The Heritage School, Rohini, Delhi. We are thankful to the Director General, Armed Force Medical Services, Ministry of Defence (M-Block), New Delhi for extending his help to conduct an interview of Surgeon Lieutenant Commander, Wahida Prism (Lesson 26); State Project Directors, SSA, Uttar Pradesh and Andhra Pradesh for providing text material on Itr (Lesson 11) and Pochampalli (Lesson 23) respectively; the teachers of K. V. Assam, Ms Bulbul (Dhuliajan) and Ms V.D. Sharma (Namroop) for providing material on Bihu (Lesssson 20) and the photograph on page 170. We thank Mamta Pandya, CEE, Ahmedabad and Neeta Beri, New Delhi for preparing the English version of the book.

We are specially grateful to K.K. Vashishtha, *Professor and Head*, Department of Elementary Education, NCERT who has extended every possible help in developing this book. We also express our gratitude to Shveta Uppal, Chief Editor, NCERT for going through the book and giving useful suggestions. We also acknowledge the contribution of Sushma Jairath, *Reader*, Department of Women Studies and Kiran Devendra, *Professor*, DEE, NCERT for editing manuscript from the gender perspective. We are grateful to Shakambar Dutt, *Incharge Computer Station*, DEE; Vijay Kumar, *DTP Operator*; Shreshtha Vats and Deepti Sharma, *Copy Editors*; Shashi Devi, *Proof Reader* in shaping the book. The efforts of the Publication Department, NCERT in bringing out this publication are also appreciated.

Contents

	Foreword	*iii*
	A Note for the Teachers and Parents	*v*
1.	Going to School	1
2.	Ear to Ear	11
3.	A Day with Nandu	21
4.	The Story of Amrita	31
5.	Anita and the Honeybees	38
6.	Omana's Journey	47
7.	From the Window	53
8.	Reaching Grandmother's House	60
9.	Changing Families	66
10.	Hu Tu Tu, Hu Tu Tu	77
11.	The Valley of Flowers	84
12.	Changing Times	96
13.	A River's Tale	106
14.	Basva's Farm	113
15.	From Market to Home	119
16.	A Busy Month	127
17.	Nandita in Mumbai	137

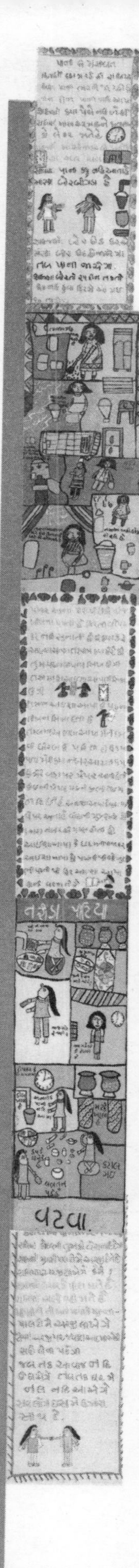

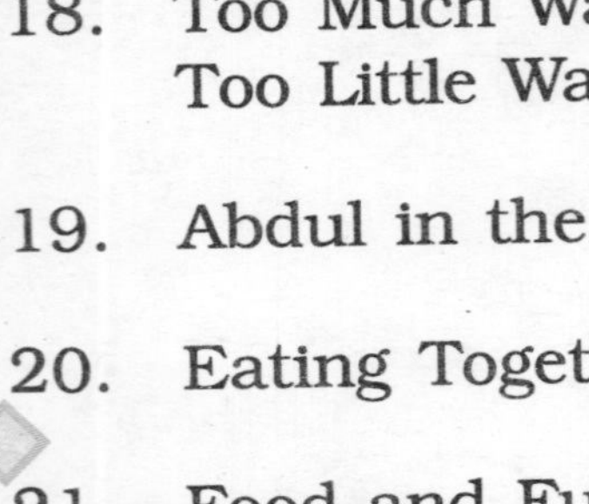

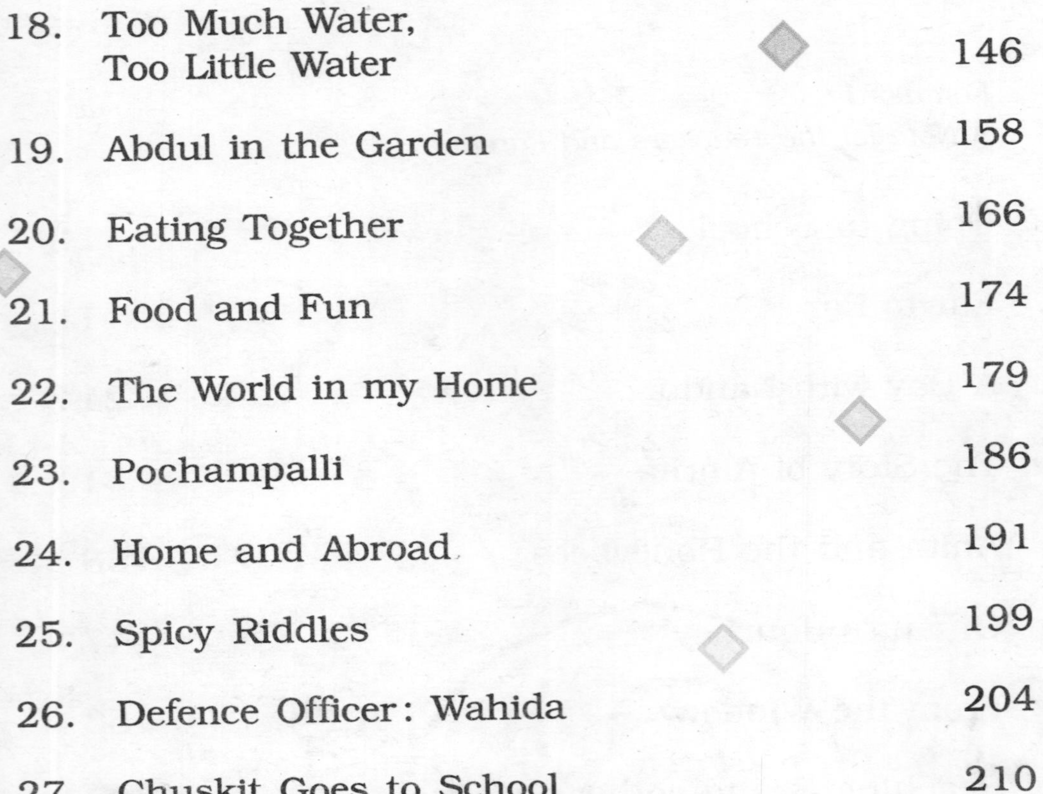

18. Too Much Water, Too Little Water 146

19. Abdul in the Garden 158

20. Eating Together 166

21. Food and Fun 174

22. The World in my Home 179

23. Pochampalli 186

24. Home and Abroad 191

25. Spicy Riddles 199

26. Defence Officer: Wahida 204

27. Chuskit Goes to School 210

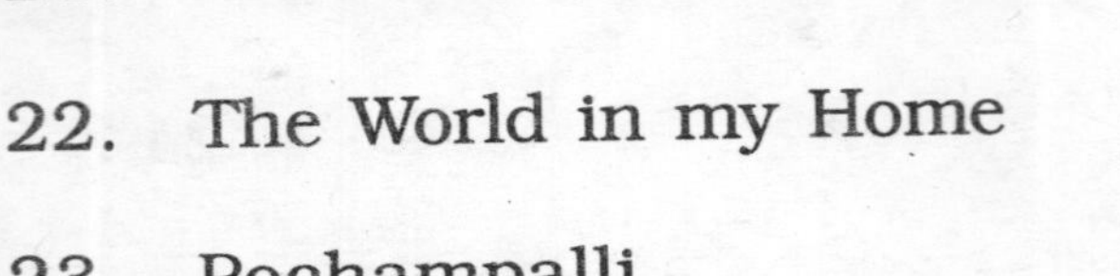

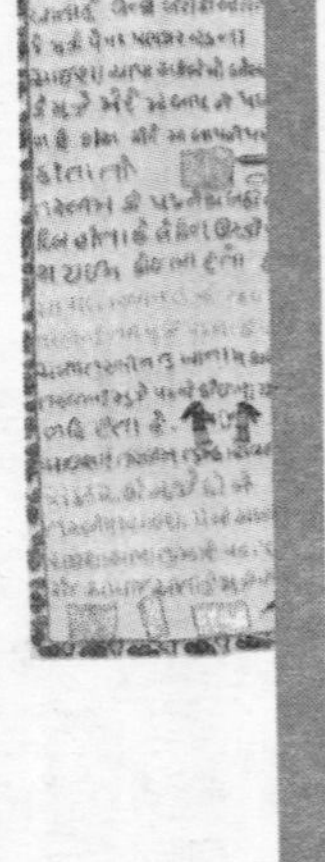

Chapter 1
Going to School

Let us meet some children and see how they reach school.

Bamboo Bridge

It rains so much where we live. Sometimes after the rain, there is knee-high water everywhere. But that does not stop us from getting to school. We hold our books in one hand and bamboo with the other. We quickly cross the bamboo and rope bridge to reach school.

Try these

- Collect some bricks. Lay them on the ground in a line as shown in the picture. Try walking on them. Was it easy ?
- Make a small bridge by tying 4 or 5 bamboo poles together. Ask your teacher to help you. Now walk on your bridge. How did you feel? Did you fall down? If you walk like this a few times, you will start finding it easy.
  - Do you think it would be easier to walk on this bridge barefoot or with shoes or slippers ? Why ?

The Trolley

Everyday we have to cross the river to get to school. The river is wide and deep. There is a strong iron rope across the river. On both the sides it is tied tightly with strong trees or rocks. There is a trolley (an open box made of wood) attached with the rope. Four or five of us sit in the trolley. A pulley helps the trolley to move across the rope. We reach the other side of the river in a short time.

Let us do

Observe pictures 1 and 2. In the pictures, children are pulling the buckets from the well. Can you tell the difference in both the pictures? Which would be easier – using the pulley or not using it to lift things?

1

2

- Look around you – where all do you see the use of pulleys? List them.
- With the help of a pulley, try and lift various things, as shown in the picture.

Cement Bridge

We often need to go across some water bodies, so we use bridges. These are made of cement, bricks and iron rods. The bridge may also have steps.

- How is this bridge different from a bamboo bridge?

  It's easier to cross.

- How many people do you think can cross the bridge at one time?

  10 people

You have seen how children use different kinds of bridges to cross rivers and other uneven areas to reach school.

- If you had a chance, which bridge would you like to use? Why?

  Cemant because I am prity sure it's easier to cross.

- Do you have to cross any bridge on the way to your school? If yes, what is the bridge like?

  NO I dont have to cross.

- Find out from your grandparents, what kinds of bridges were there when they were young.

  bamboo bridge

Is there any bridge near your house? Find out more about the bridge.

- Where is the bridge – over water, over a road, between two mountains or somewhere else?

  ___

- Who all use the bridge? Is it used by people on foot and also by vehicles and animals?

  ___

- Does the bridge seem to be old or is it new?

  ___

- Find out what materials are used in making this bridge. List some of them.

  ___

- Draw a picture of the bridge in your notebook. Do not forget to draw the train, vehicles, animals or people who cross the bridge.
- Imagine what difficulties there would be, if the bridge was not there?

Let us find out some other ways by which children get to school.

Vallam

In some parts of Kerala, we use a *vallam* (small wooden boat) to reach school.

- Have you seen any other kind of boats? ______________

- Can you think of other ways by which we can travel on water?

____

Camel-cart

Rajasthan

We live in the desert. There is sand all around. It gets very hot in the day. We ride in a camel-cart to reach school.

- Have you ever sat in a camel-cart or horse carriage (tonga)? Where? Did you climb on it yourself, or did someone help you?

____

____

____

- How did you feel riding in the cart? Also share your experience in the class also.

Bullock-cart

We ride in our bullock-cart, going slowly through the green fields. If it is too sunny or raining, we use our umbrellas.

Village in the plains

For the Teacher: How do animal feel when made to pull cart. Discuss issues to develop sensitivity towards animals.

- Do you have bullock-carts where you live?

- Does it have a roof?

- What kind of wheels do they have?

- Make a drawing of the cart in your notebook.

Bicycle ride

We ride our bicycles on the long road to school. At first, girls here did not go to school, because it was too far. But now groups of 7-8 girls easily ride even through the difficult roads.

- Can you ride a bicycle? If yes, who taught you to ride?

- How many children come on bicycles to your school?

Jugad – What a Vehicle!

Look at our special transport. It sounds *phut-phut-phut* when it runs. Is it not something special! The front looks like a motorcycle but the carriage at the back is made out of planks of wood.

- Do you have such vehicles in your area?

  ____

- What do you call them in your area?

  ____

- Would you like to ride in something like this? Why?

  ____

- Can you tell why it is called *jugad*?

  ____

- The *jugad* has been made by putting together parts from other vehicles or machines. For example, tyres, engine, wooden parts from different things. That is why it is called 'jugad' (putting together). Why don't you also try to make something new by putting together parts from different things.

Can you think of a place where none of these vehicles can reach? Yes, there are such places!

Children cross the Jungle

We have to go through a thick forest to reach school. At some places, it is so thick that even sunlight does not pass through. It is also very silent there, you can only hear the sounds of different birds and other creatures.

- Have you ever been in a thick jungle or any such place?

  ____

- Write your experiences in your notebook.
- Can you recognise some birds by their sounds? Can you imitate the sounds of some birds? Do it.

Moving on the Snow

See, how we reach school! We go to school through miles of snow. We hold hands and walk carefully. If the snow is soft, our feet sink into it. When the snow is frozen, we may slip and fall.

- Have you ever seen so much snow? Where? In films or somewhere else?

  ____

  ____

Northern Hills

- Do you think that such places have snow all the time? Why?

____

Rocky Paths

We live in the mountains. The paths are rocky and uneven. The children who live in the plains will find it difficult to walk on these. But we can easily race up and down.

Uttarakhand

No matter whether there is a dense forest, farms, mountains or snow on the way, we manage to reach school.

- Do you face difficulties on the way to your school?

____

- Which is the best month, in which you like to go to school? Why?

____

____

See Me Walk!

- Go to a ground or an open space with your friends. Act the way you will walk in these situations.
  - The ground is made of soft and smooth rose petals.
  - The ground is covered with thorns and there is tall grass on the sides.
  - The ground is covered with snow.

Was there a difference in the way you walked each time? Discuss.

From Children's Pen

Failed in the test – 30 rulers

Fooled around in the test – 15 rulers

Homework not done? – 8 rulers

Nails, teeth, dress not clean – 30 sit ups

Having fun in class when teacher is out – Stand on one leg for two hours.

Not back in class after the recess – Stand on the bench with your hands up in the air for one hour.

– Sagar Mishra, Class V
Chakmak, August 2006
Devas, Madhya Pradesh

Talk about it

- Do you also have punishment in your school? What kind?
- Do you think that punishment should be there in schools?
- Is punishment the only solution to misdeeds? Make some rules for school to prevent misdeeds.

- Draw a picture of your 'dream school' in your notebook and write about it.

For the teacher: The purpose behind giving this column is to totally discourage punishments in schools. Discuss this issue sensitively in the class. Encourage the students for self discipline.

Who has got my ears?

Are these animals looking funny? The artist has drawn wrong ears on the heads of the animals. Give correct ears to the animals in the space given below.

Animal	Ear	Animal	Ear
Elephant	Mouse	Dog	________
Rabbit	________	Buffalo	________
Mouse	________	Deer	________
Giraffe	________		

Different animals have different kinds of ears. Among the animals given below, which one have ears that you can see? In which animal you can not see the ears? Write in the table below.

Deer	**Frog**	**Fish**	**Ant**	**Crow**
Tiger	**Sparrow**	**Buffalo**	**Snake**	**Lizard**
Pig	**Duck**	**Giraffe**	**Elephant**	**Cat**

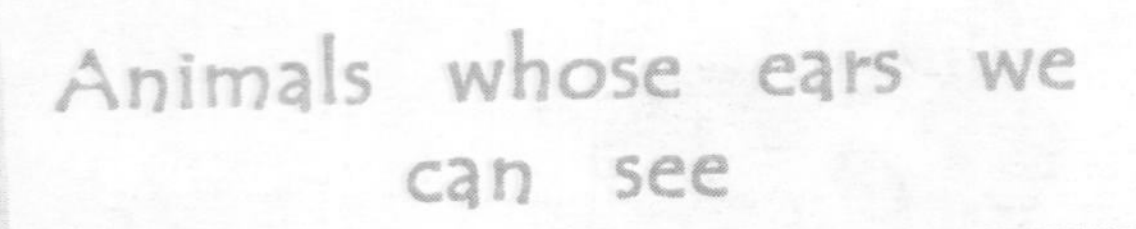

Animals whose ears we can see		Animals whose ears we can not see	
____________	____________	____________	____________
____________	____________	____________	____________
____________	____________	____________	____________

Do you think that the animals whose ears we can not see, really do not have ears?

Let us observe this picture.

Name the animals in the picture.

Can you see their ears?

They all have ears, even though we can not see them.

- Find out some other animals which have ears that we can not see. Write their names.

____

Read and Write

- An animal with ears like fan ______________
- An animal with ears like leaves ______________
- An animal with ears on the top of its head ______________
- An animal with ears on both sides of its head ______________

You know very well that ears help us to hear. In some animals you can see the ears, in some you can not. We can not see a bird's ears. A bird has tiny holes on both sides of its head. Generally, the holes are covered with feathers. They help the bird to hear.

If you look carefully, you will see tiny holes on a lizard's head. These are its ears.

A crocodile also has ears like this, but we can not see them easily.

Whose Skin

Now you know how to recognise animals by their ears. Let us see if we can recognise animals by their skin.

Match the animals shown here with the pictures of their skin. Make the correct pattern of the skin on the picture of each animal.

The different patterns on the animals are due to the hair on their skin.

Have you ever seen an animal without hair or whose hair have been removed? Imagine how the animal would look if it did not have any hair on its skin. There would be no patterns!

You might have seen some of the animals given below.

Fox	**Elephant**	**Sparrow**	**Pigeon**
Frog	**Crow**	**Peacock**	**Pig**
Mouse	**Cat**	**Buffalo**	**Duck**
Hen	**Camel**	**Lizard**	**Cow**

Put the names of the animals in the table below.

Ears can be seen	Has hair on skin	Ears can not be seen	Has feathers on skin

In which list did you put the cow and the buffalo? From a distance, can you see the hair on their skin? Try to go near one of them. Could you see the hair?

If you were to meet an elephant, would you dare to touch it? Do you know that an elephant also has hair on its skin.

For the Teacher: Discuss more details of mentioned animals in this chapter such as their food habits, habitats, etc. Develop sensitivity towards animals.

Can you tell which of the animals mentioned in the list lay eggs? Find out and write the names of these animals in the green box.

Which of the animals in the list give birth to babies? Write their names in the red box.

Now, look again at the table on the previous page. Draw a line under the names of animals whose names are in the green box. Put a circle around the names of those animals whose names are in the red box.

So, what did you note? Those animals whose ears you can see have hair on their body. These animals give birth to the

young ones. Those animals that do not have ears on the outside, do not have hair on their body. These animals lay eggs.

- Have you seen animals around your house or school that have small babies? Write their names in your notebook.
- Have you ever kept a pet? Does anyone you know keep a pet?
- Find out more about the pet.
  - Which animal is it?

    ____

  - Does it have a name? What is it?

    ____

  - Who gave it this name?

    ____

  - What does it like to eat?

    ____

  - How many times a day is it given food?

    ____

  - When does it sleep? For how long does it sleep?

    ____

  - Is there any special way to look after this animal? How?

    ____

    ____

  - Does it get angry? When? How do you know it is angry?

    ____

    ____

- Does it have hair or feathers on its skin?

____

- Can you see its ears?

____

- Is it a baby or a young animal or a full grown animal?

____

- Will this pet animal lay eggs or give birth to babies?

____

- Does it have young ones?

____

- Draw a picture of this animal and colour it. Give it a name of your own choice.

Look at this picture. Colour the parts which have even numbers (2, 4, 6, 8...). What do you see? Find out the name of the animal.

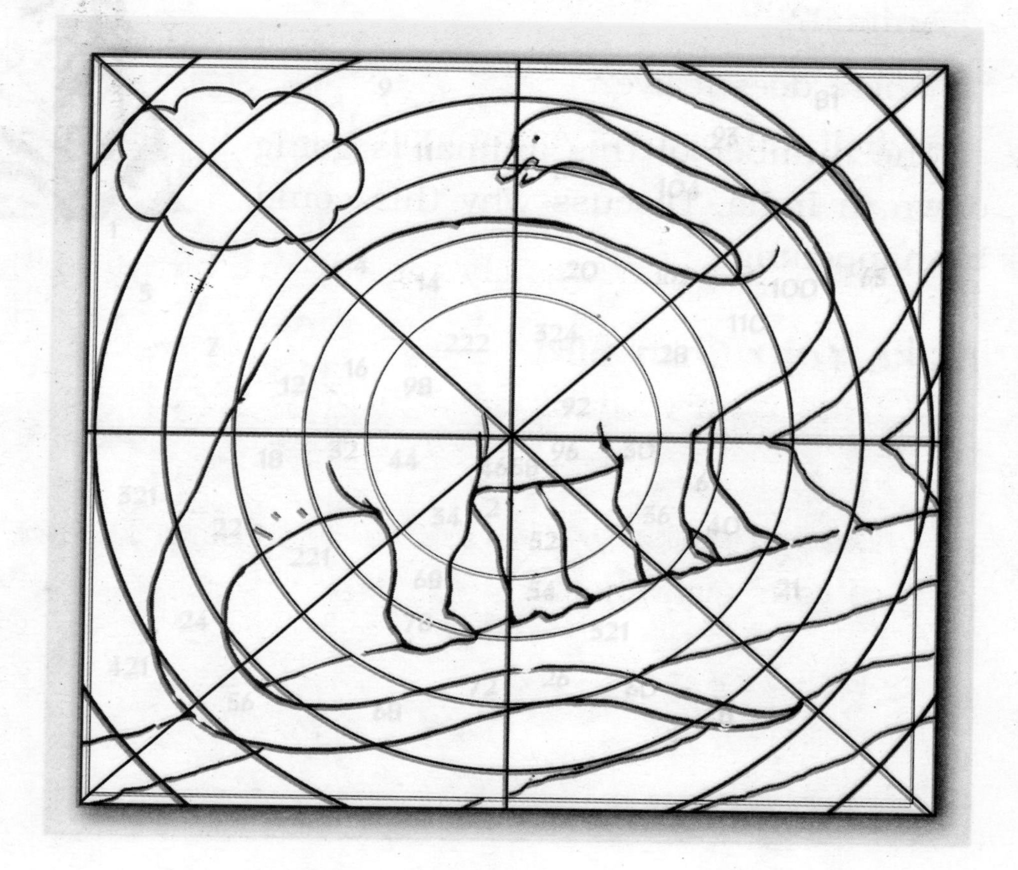

Many many years ago there were dinosaurs on earth, but not any more. Now we see them in films, photos and books. Find out more about dinosaurs and share with your friends.

Have you seen any animal that looks a little like dinosaur? Do you know its name?

Find out from your elders.

For the teacher: Chidren may name many different animals that they think resemble the dinosaur. All answers are acceptable. You can create and organise more such activities in the class.

- Look at this animal. Write its name. Do you know that this is our National Animal?
- Where does it live?

The number of this animal is going down in India. Discuss why this could be happening?

Make Your Own Bird

For the teacher: For making the paper bird it will be useful if the paper used has different colours on both sides.

Chapter 3

A Day with Nandu

Nandu Wakes Up

Nandu woke up and opened his eyes. For a few seconds he was not sure where he was. It seemed to him that he was surrounded by a forest of big grey tree trunks. He blinked his eyes and looked around. Oh! There was *Amma*.

The grey forest that he had imagined he was in, was actually the legs and trunks of his family members.

The sun was overhead and it was getting hot. *Nani ma* trumpetted – made a loud sound. *Nani ma* is the oldest in this herd of elephants. She started moving towards the jungle. The other female elephants saw her and started to follow her. Nandu also went with them.

For the teacher: Mother's mother is called *nani ma*. Ask children what they call their mother's mother.

When they reached the jungle, the members of the herd started spreading out. Each member went to eat her favourite leaves and twigs. After they had eaten, the herd moved towards the river. The baby elephants enjoyed playing in the water. The mothers lay down in the water and mud on the river bank.

Do you know that an adult elephant can eat more than 100 kilograms of leaves and twigs in one day? Elephants do not rest very much. They sleep for only two to four hours in a day. Elephants love to play with mud and water. The mud keeps their skin cool. Their big ears also work like fans. The elephants flap these to keep themselves cool.

Find out

- Nandu is only three months old, but he weighs 200 kilograms. What is your weight?

  ____

- Can you find out – the weight of how many children like you will add up to Nandu's weight?

  ____

Fun and Games

Nandu saw his brothers and sisters pulling each other's tails. He thought, "I better not go near them. What if they fall on me? I am still small." He quietly went and stood near his mother.

Amma gently pushed Nandu towards the water, as if she was telling him to go and play. Nandu loved to play in the water. His cousins were already there. Just as he reached near, a strong fountain of water fell on his head. He got wet. Oh, this was the work of his naughty cousins. Nandu joined them in the game.

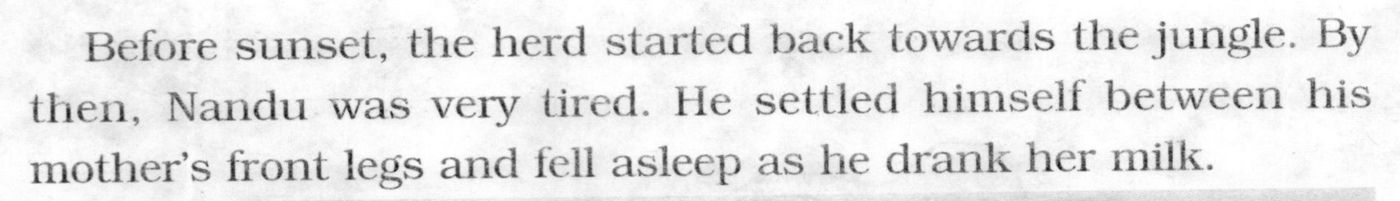

Before sunset, the herd started back towards the jungle. By then, Nandu was very tired. He settled himself between his mother's front legs and fell asleep as he drank her milk.

You have read about Nandu and the elephant herd. An elephant herd has mainly females and baby elephants. The oldest female is the leader of the herd. A herd may have 10 to 12 female elephants and young ones. Male elephants live in the herd till they are 14–15 years old. Then they leave their herd and move around alone. Nandu will also leave his herd when he is that old.

Like elephants, some other animals also live together in groups. These animal groups are called herds. Animals in herds usually move around together, searching for food.

- If you were Nandu, and you lived in a herd, what kind of things would you do?

  ____

  ____

  ____

- In the elephant herd, the oldest female elephant decides everything. Who takes decisions in your family?

  ____

  ____

  ____

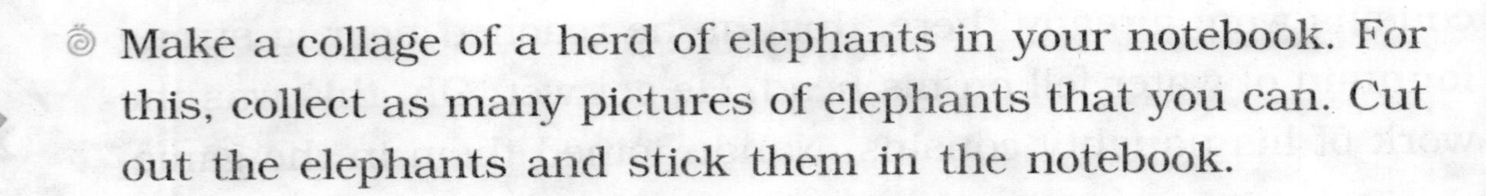

- Make a collage of a herd of elephants in your notebook. For this, collect as many pictures of elephants that you can. Cut out the elephants and stick them in the notebook.

- Nandu did things that he liked to do. If you could spend a whole day with your friends, what all would you do?

- Find out and write, which other animals live in herds.

- Do you also live in a group? Do you like to live together like that? Why would you like or not like to live in a group?

Why I would like	Why I would not like

- How do elephants feel when they kept in chains? Discuss and share your feelings.

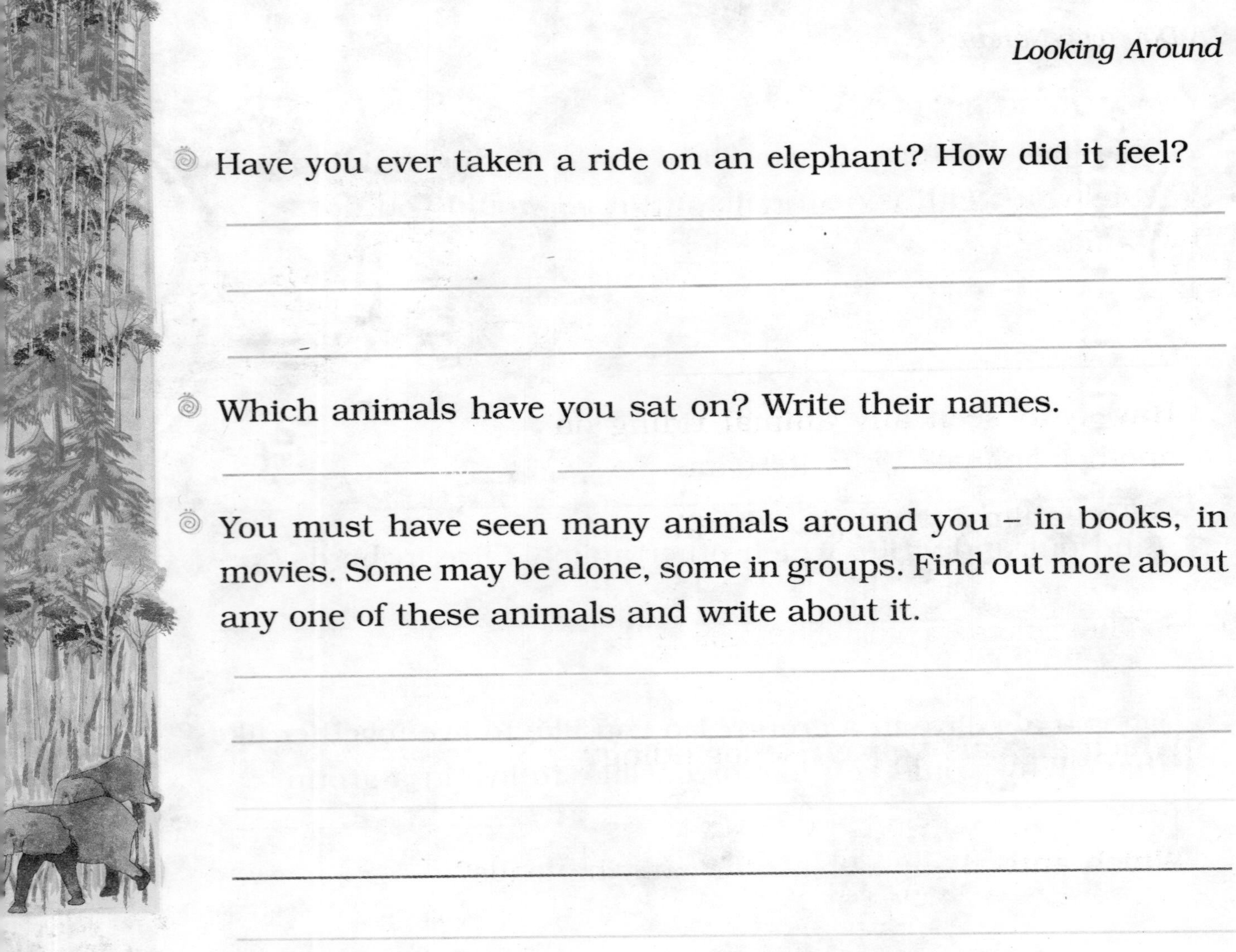

- Have you ever taken a ride on an elephant? How did it feel?

____

____

____

- Which animals have you sat on? Write their names.

______________ ______________ ______________

- You must have seen many animals around you – in books, in movies. Some may be alone, some in groups. Find out more about any one of these animals and write about it.

____

____

____

____

____

Think and Write

Why do you think the egret is sitting on the buffalo?

____

____

- Have you seen any animal riding on another animal? Write its name.
  - The animal which is riding.

    ____

  - The animal which gives the ride.

    ____

- Which animals do we use for riding?

  ____

- Which animals do we use for carrying loads?

  ____

  ____

Make Your Own Elephant

- Copy the drawing of the elephant given on the next page in a bigger size on a thick sheet of paper.
  - Make small cuts where it says "cut" ()in the picture. Be careful not to cut off the part.
  - Fold along the dotted lines [..........]
  - Fold the part with [////////] pattern and push them underneath.
  - Cut out the tail and stick it on.

Your elephant is ready.

Colour and decorate it.

Put up an exhibition in class of all the paper-elephants that you have made.

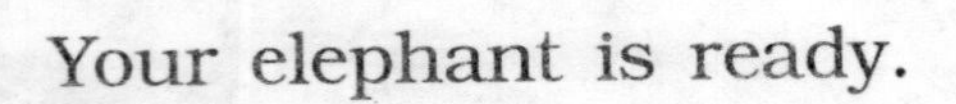

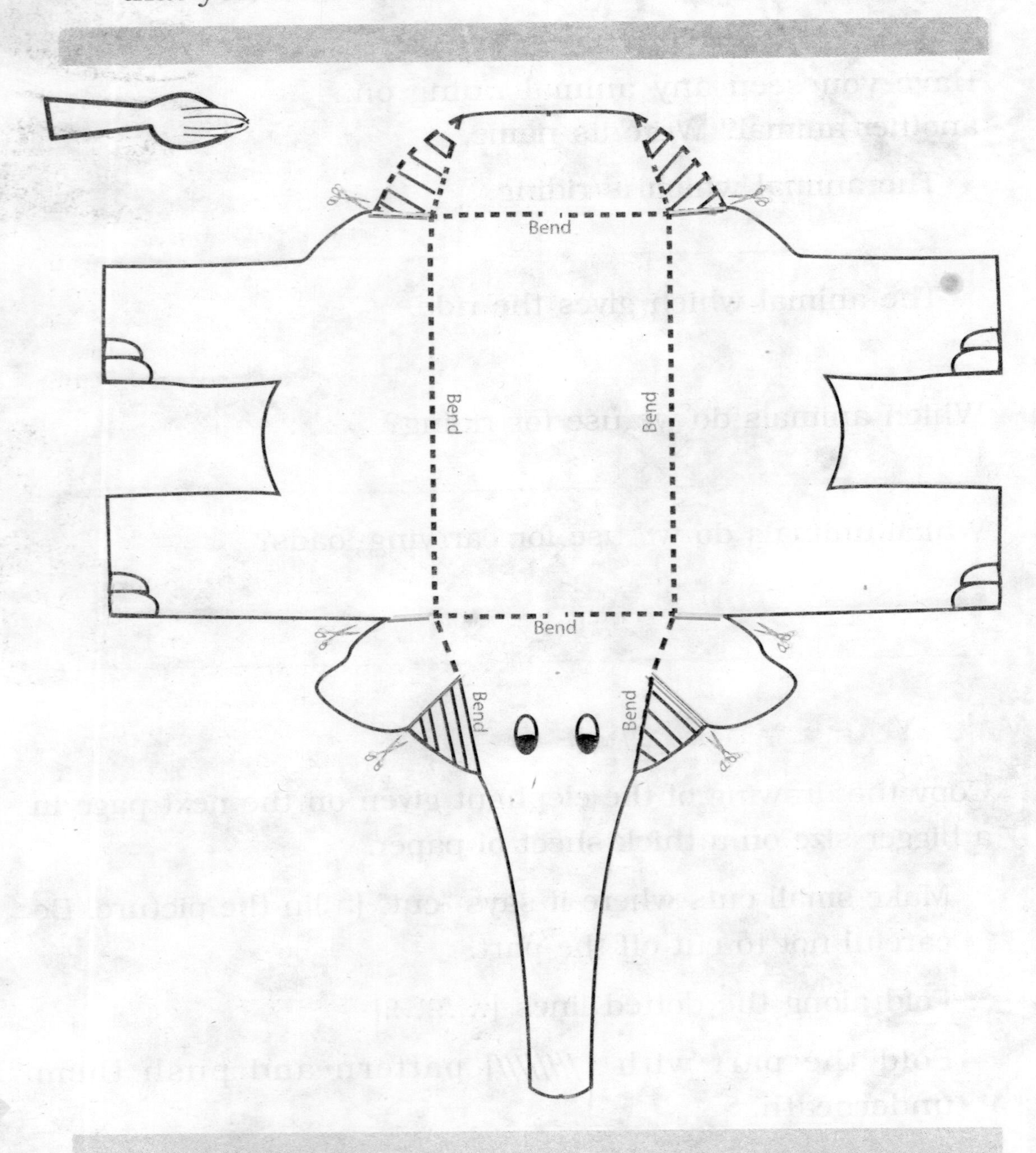

What do They Say?

Look at these pictures and read what these animals are sharing with their friends. Discuss these narratives sensitively in the class.

The basket is the only home I have. I have forgotten what it is like in the open jungle and fresh air. For me it is only the basket and the snake charmer!

You see me in circus – dancing and jumping through rings of fire. You clap and enjoy. Do you think that I also enjoy all this? If I do not do this I will get no food, only get a beating!

You have only seen how fast I run. Have you seen my 'shoes'? Do you know how much pain I get when they fix the horseshoes to my hooves?

They make us dance and dance and dance. Even if we don't want to, or we are in pain. That too, with an empty stomach!

Meow! Meow! Meow! I can just roam around everywhere. Children love me a lot. They pat me and also give me milk.

Gurtargoo! Gurtargoo! Do you know people specially call out to me to feed me with grain.

Discuss

- You have read what these animals say. Why do you think that some of them are sad?
- How do you think they are different – the monkeys that dance to entertain people and the monkeys that are free?

How many legs does this elephant have?

Do you know?

Elephants help each other when in trouble. They join together to care for and rescue their young ones.

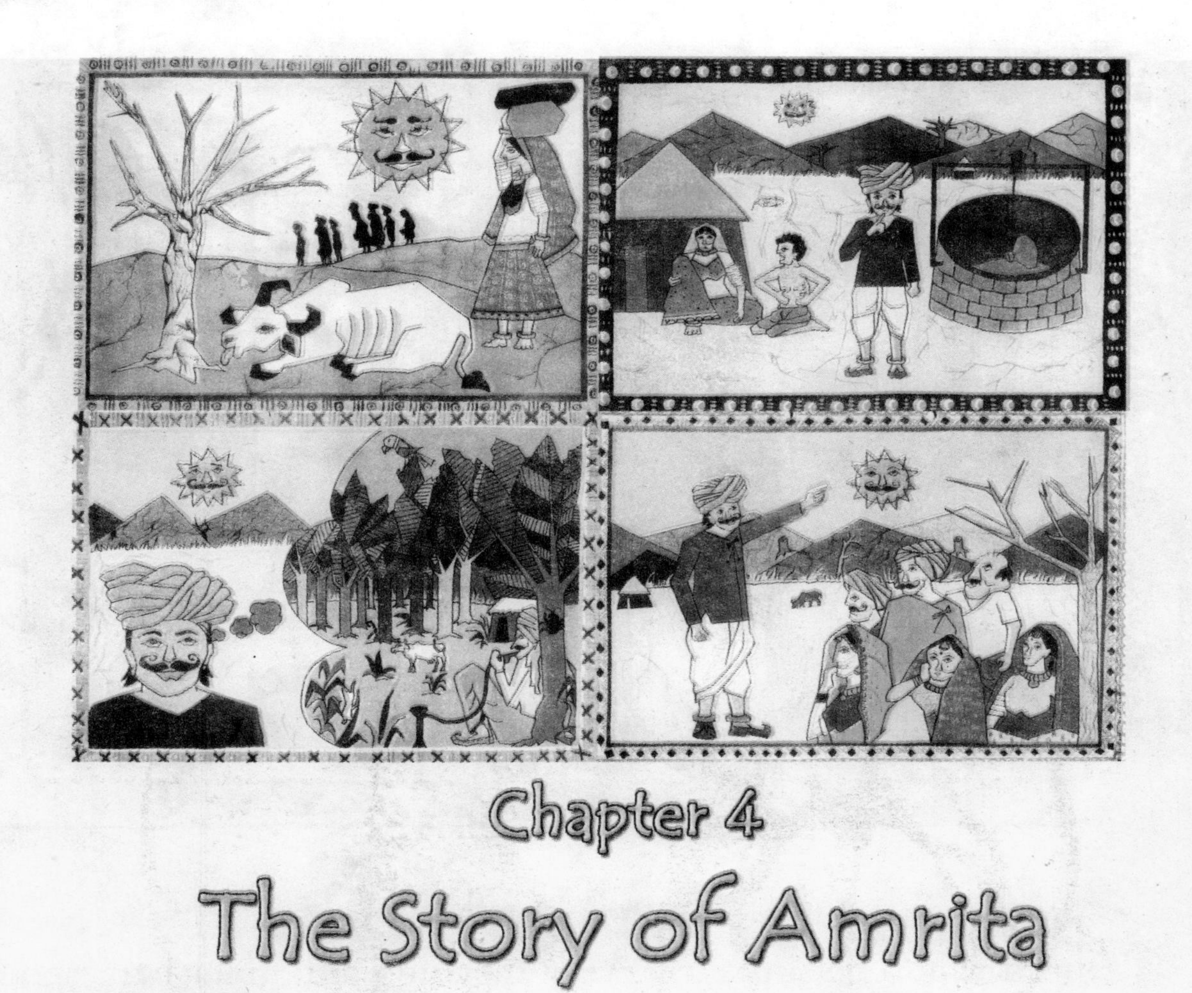

Chapter 4
The Story of Amrita

This is a true story from long long ago. Almost three hundred years ago, in a village called Khejadli, lived Amrita. Khejadli village is near Jodhpur in Rajasthan. The village got its name because of the many *Khejadi* trees that grew there.

The people of this village took great care of the plants, trees and animals. Goats, deer, hares and peacocks roamed fearlessly there. The people of the village remembered what their elders used to tell them. They used to say, "*Agar perh hain to hum hain.* Plants and animals can survive without us, but we can not survive without them."

For the teacher: Encourage children to locate Rajasthan on the map of India.

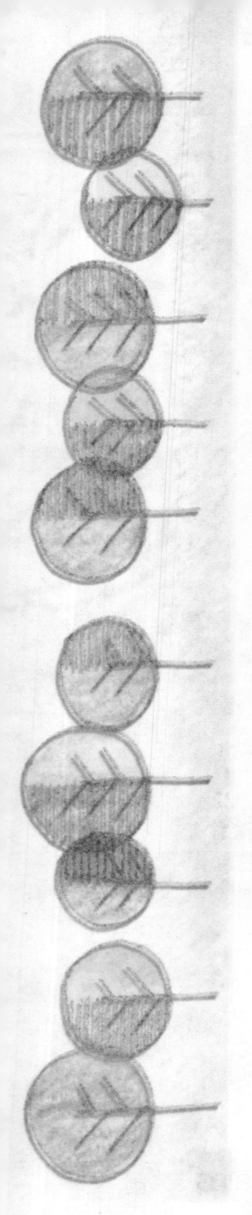

Amrita's Friends

Amrita would get up early every morning and greet her friends – the trees. She would choose a special tree for the day. She would put her arms around the tree trunk and whisper to the tree, "Friend, you are strong and beautiful. You care for us. Thank you tree. I love you very much. Give your strength to me also."

Like Amrita, the other children also had their special trees. They would play for hours in the shade of the trees.

- Is there a place near your house, school or along the road side, where trees have been planted?
- Why were they planted there?

____

- Have you seen anyone taking care of the trees? Who does this?

  ____

- Have you seen fruits on any of the tree? Who eats these fruits?

  ____

  ____

- Lalita feels that grass and small plants growing near her school wall have not been planted by anyone. Do you know of any place where grass, small plants or trees are growing on their own without being planted by anyone?

  ____

- Why do you feel they are growing on their own?

  ____

  ____

Trees in Danger

Time went by. Amrita was now grown up. One day she went to greet her trees. She saw that there were some strangers in her village. They had axes with them. They said that the King had sent them to cut trees for wood. The wood was needed for building the King's palace.

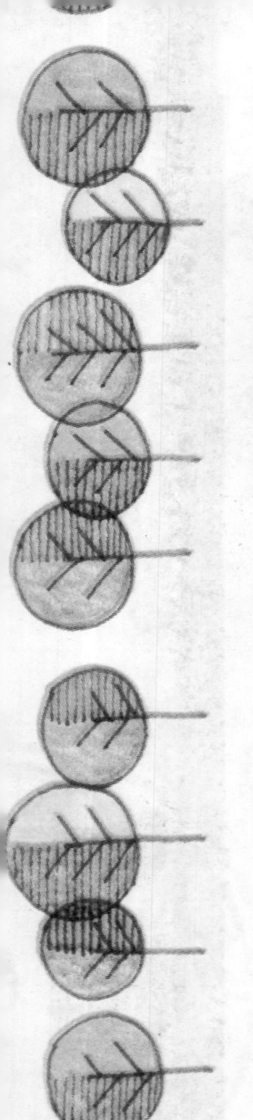

Amrita was shocked. She went to the tree that the men were about to cut. She put her arms around the tree and hugged it tightly. The men shouted and threatened her, but Amrita did not let go of the tree. The King's men had to follow his order. They had to cut the tree. On seeing this, Amrita's daughters and hundreds of villagers–old and young–hugged the trees to protect them. Many people including Amrita and her daughters died to save the trees.

When the King heard of this, he could not believe that people gave up their life for trees. He visited the village himself. There he learned about villagers' respect for trees and animals.

- Do you remember what the elders of this village used to say?
- Do you think we could survive if there were no trees and no animals? Discuss this in your class.

The Village is Protected

The villagers' strong feelings for trees affected the King greatly. He ordered that from then on, no tree would be cut and no animal would be harmed in that area. Even today, almost three hundred years later, the people of this area, called Bishnois, continue to

protect plants and animals. Even though in the middle of the desert, this area is green and animals roam freely without fear.

- Do you remember that in Class III, you had made a tree your friend? How is your friend now?
  - Why don't you make a new friend this year? Have you seen how your friends–the trees, change in some ways, in different months of a year.

Write about any one tree.

- Does the tree flower?

  ___

- Do the flowers remain on the tree throughout the year?

  ___

- In which month do the leaves fall?

  ___

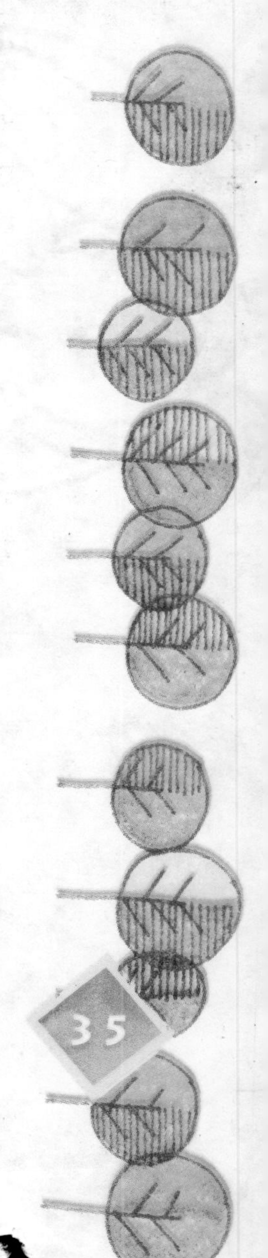

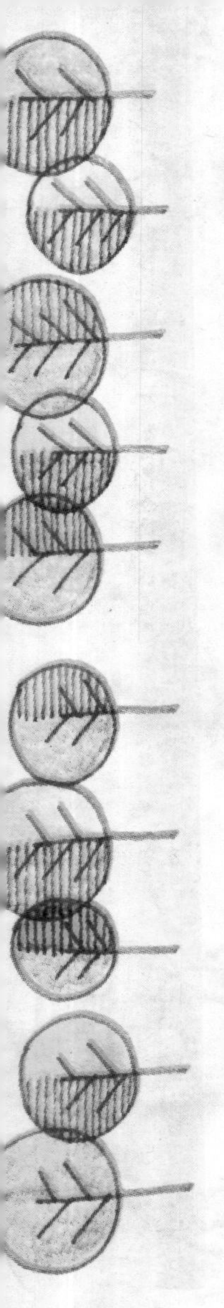

- Do fruits grow on the tree?

____

- In which months do they grow?

____

- Have you eaten these fruits?

____

Sometime back you have read in the newspapers or seen on TV how some film actors had to face legal action for hunting a blackbuck.

Discuss

- Why do people hunt?
- There are rules against hunting of some animals. People can be punished for hunting. Why do you think there is this punishment?

____

Talk to your grandparents and find out –

- Which birds did they see around them when they were of your age?

____

____

- Have the number of some of these birds become less?

____

- Are there some birds or animals which they can not see any more?

____

- Shanti's grandfather told her that when he was a small child he saw more birds like sparrows and *mynah* than he sees today. Can you make two guesses why their numbers have become less?

___

___

___

The *Khejadi* tree was the most common tree that grew in Amrita's village. Which kind of trees can you see a lot of, in your area? Name two such trees.

- Find out more about these trees from your elders.

___

___

___

The *Khejadi* tree is found mainly in desert areas. It can grow without much water. Its bark is used for making medicines. People cook and eat its fruits (beans). Its wood is such that it will not be affected by insects. Animals in this area eat the leaves of the *Khejadi*. And children like you, play in its shade.

For the teacher: Encourage children to ask their elders about animals and insects. Discuss with the children about the reducing number of birds due to changes in the environment.

Chapter 5
Anita and the Honeybees

My name is Anita Khushwaha. I live in Bochaha village. This is in Muzzafarpur District in Bihar. I stay with my parents and two younger brothers. I study in college. Besides studying, I teach young children. I also keep honeybees.

All this has not been easy for me. When I was young, I used to spend all my time with my goats as they grazed for food. I always wanted to go to school but my parents did not like the idea of girls going to school.

---

* This is a true story. Anita Khushwaha is a 'Girl Star'. 'Girl Stars' is a project which tells extraordinary tales of ordinary girls who have changed their life by going to school.

* Encourage children to locate Bihar on the map of India.

A Dream of School

One day I peeped into the school in our village. I could not stay away. I silently went and sat down behind the children. I felt so happy. I went home and picked up courage to talk to my parents about going to school. But they told me clearly that I could not do so. That day, I cried and cried.

One of the teachers in my village explained to my parents why it is important to study. The teacher told them that they would not have to pay anything for my education upto Class VIII. The teacher said that it was the right of every child to go to school. Somehow my parents agreed. I started going to school. I did not get high marks, but I always asked many questions!

- Find out how much money do you spend in one year for various school related things.

Things	Money Spent
1. Travel to school and back	
2. Notebooks	
3. Pens-Pencils/Stationery	
4. Uniforms	
5. School bag	
6. Lunch Box	
7. Shoes	
8. Other Things (i)	
(ii)	
Total	

- How much money did you spend on your books this year?

____

- What kind of a school uniform would you like to wear? Draw a picture of it in your notebook and colour it.
- Make two groups in the class. Debate the topic – 'We should have uniforms in school.'

Staying in School

Time passed, and soon I completed Class V. I knew that we would need to spend more in Class VI. My parents said that it was time for me to leave school, but I wanted to study more. I found a way to do this. I started to teach younger children. From the money that I got, I was able to continue my own studies.

One Sweet Memory

I remember some older boys in my village also used to teach young children. They did not like it when I started teaching. They started to scold and scare the children, so that they would not come to me. For some time, all the children except two, stopped coming to me. But soon they all came back because I used to teach them with love and care.

Let us talk

- Do you know someone who wanted to study, but could not do so? Talk about them in the class.

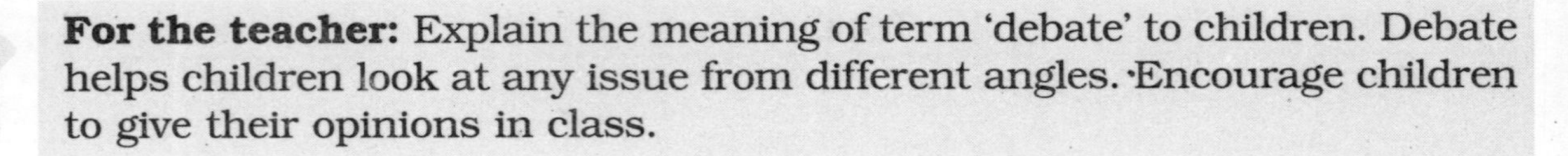

For the teacher: Explain the meaning of term 'debate' to children. Debate helps children look at any issue from different angles. Encourage children to give their opinions in class.

- Every child has a right to free education upto Class VIII. Do you think that all children are able to study up to Class VIII? Discuss.

Slowly I started talking to other parents in the village about sending their daughters to school. My parents also started helping me in my work. My mother used to do all the house work so that I could get more time to study.

A Secret
I learnt how to ride a motor-cycle. I did not tell anyone. I fell down and got hurt many times, but I was happy!

From School to Bee-keeping

There are many litchi trees in our area. Honeybees are attracted to the litchi flowers. Many people do bee-keeping and collect honey. I thought that I could also do this. I joined a course run by the government to learn about this. I was the only girl in this course. During my training I found that honeybees lay their eggs from October to December. This was the best time to start bee-keeping.

- Have you seen any insects near flowers? Find out their names and write.

  ____

- Draw and colour their pictures in the notebook.
- Why do you think they come to the flowers? Find out.

  ____

  ____

- When honeybees fly, there is a kind of sound. Can you try to copy this sound?

Becoming a Bee-keeper

I completed my bee-keeping course. But I did not have money to keep my own bees and start work. I continued to teach and with time could collect Rs. 5000. With this money, I bought two boxes for keeping bees. Each box costs Rs. 2000. With the remaining money, I bought sugar to make the syrup for honeybees, and medicines to clean the beehives.

That was in September. By December, I had so many bees that I had to buy two more boxes. I was still learning about bee-keeping. Many times, the bees would sting me and my hands and face would get swollen. It would pain a lot. How could I complain to anybody? I myself had decided to do this work.

Find out

- What do people in your area put on the part of the body where the bee has stung?
- Draw a picture of a honeybee in your notebook. Colour it and give it a name.

The litchi trees come to flower in February. I put all my four boxes near the litchi orchards. I got 12 kilograms of honey from each box. I sold this honey in the market. This was my first earning from my bees. Now I have 20 boxes.

- What will be the total cost of Anita's 20 boxes?

Every day I cycle to my college. My college is in the town, five kilometres away. When I go to college, my mother prepares the syrup for the bees. My father looks after the bees and takes the honey out of the boxes.

Now you also know a lot about Anita.

Anita is known by everyone in all the villages nearby. She goes to all the village meetings and talks about how important it is for everyone to study. Sometimes people make fun of her, but Anita knows what she wants to do. She does exactly what she wants to.

Anita wants to become a wholesaler so that she can help the villagers to get the right price for their honey.

Find out

- Anita and others in her village get Rs.35 for one kilogram of honey. How much does one kilogram of honey cost in your town?

  ____

- What are the different colours of honey that you have seen?

  __________ __________ __________

- Is honey used in your house? What is it used for?

  ____

Every beehive has one Queen Bee that lays eggs. There are only a few males in the hive. Most of the bees in the hive are worker-bees. These bees work all day. They make the hive and

For the teacher: Explain the role of wholesaler to children.

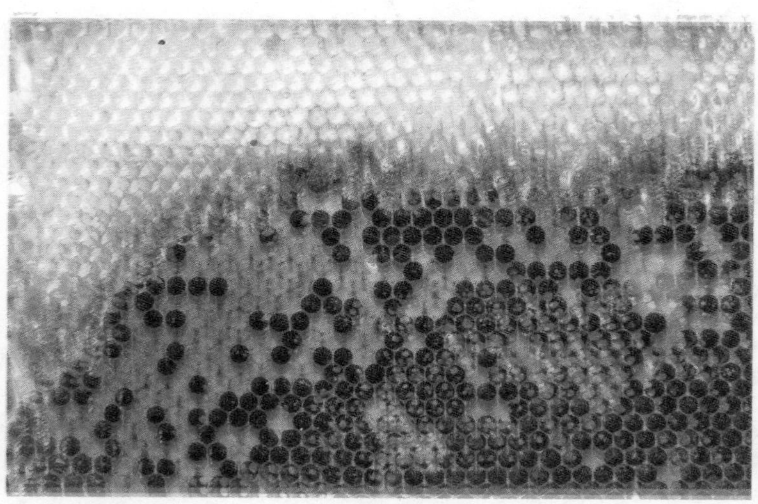

also look after the baby bees. They fly around flowers in search of nectar. They collect nectar from flowers for honey. When one bee finds flowers with nectar, it does a special kind of dance by which the other bees can know where the nectar is. The worker-bees are very important for the hive. Without worker-bees there would be neither hive nor any nectar collection. All bees in the hive would go hungry. The male bees have no special role as workers.

- Which are some other insects that live together in a group, like honeybees?

  ____

Ants live and work together like honeybees. The Queen Ant lays the eggs, the Soldier Ants look after and guard the ants' nest, Worker Ants are always busy looking for food and bringing it to the nest. Termites and wasps also live like this.

- Have you seen where ants live?

  ____

- What kind of eatables attract ants? List them.

  ____

  ____

- Look at a line of ants. What is its colour?

  ____

- Have you been bitten by an ant? What was the ant like – black or red, big or small?

  ____

- Do ants ever come near you? When?

  ____

- Look carefully at some big and small ants. How many legs does an ant have?

  Big ant ____________

  Small ant ____________

- Draw an ant in your notebook and colour it.
- While eating peanuts you probably throw away the shells. Why don't you try to make some insects by using the shells. Do not forget to colour them.

Chapter 6
Omana's Journey

Omana and her best friend Radha were very excited. They were going on a train trip to Kerala. Omana was going to her grandmother's house and Radha was going with her family for a holiday. Omana's father had gone to book train tickets for both the families.

Then, just two days before their journey, Radha fell down from her bicycle and fractured her right leg. Her leg was put in plaster. The doctor said that she should not move her leg for six weeks. Radha's family had to cancel their tickets. The two friends were very sad. They had made so many plans about what they would do together on the trip. Then Radha's Amma had an idea. "Omana, why don't you write down everything about your trip in a diary? Then when you come back Radha can read all about your trip. This way you will not forget anything and it will also help you to pass the time on the train."

Both the friends thought this was a good idea. Omana went home and found a notebook with blank pages to write all about her journey. Here are some pages from Omana's diary for you to read.

Omana's Diary

16 May

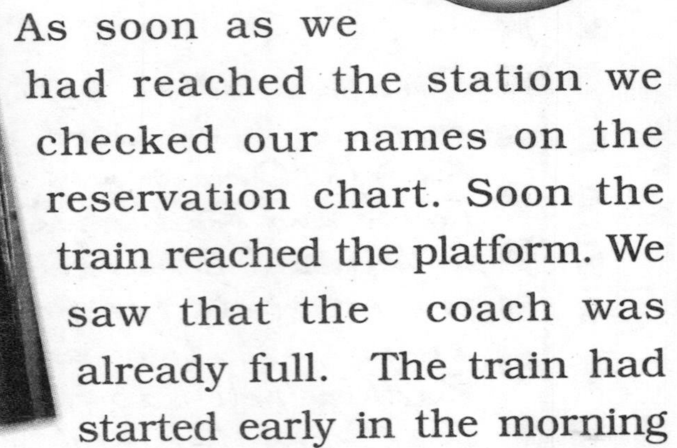

As soon as we had reached the station we checked our names on the reservation chart. Soon the train reached the platform. We saw that the coach was already full. The train had started early in the morning from Gandhidham, in Kutch. When the train came, there was so much confusion. People were getting off and others were pushing and trying to put their luggage inside, all from one door.

We somehow managed to get in, find our seats and put our luggage under them. By the time the train started, most people had found their seats and arranged their luggage. After some time the ticket collector came and checked our tickets to see that we were in our proper seats. *Amma* and *Appa* had the lower berths. Unni and I have the middle

berths. There are two college students who have the upper berths. On the other berths, there is a family with two children. They seem to be about our age. I will go and talk to them later.

Now I am sitting near the window and I have started writing about our journey, just as I had promised you. I will stop now because *Amma* has opened the tiffin box. *Amma* had packed a lot of food – *dhokla* with *chutney*, lemon rice, and some *mithai*. My mouth is watering. I will write more later.

- Why was it so crowded at the door of the coach?

  ____

  ____

- Have you ever travelled in a train? When?

  ____

  ____

- What food would you like to take with you when you travel? Why?

  ____________ ____________ ____________

  ____________ ____________ ____________

- What does the ticket-checker do?

  ____

  ____

- How will you recognise the ticket-checker?

  ____

  ____

16 May

After lunch some people slept. But I was not sleepy. I kept looking out of the window. I saw many fields, but they all were brown and dry. Sometimes we passed small villages. They seemed to be flying by. Do you know that when the train is at a very high speed things outside seem to be running in the opposite direction?

Earlier it was really hot. Now that it is evening, there is some breeze.

The sun is slowly setting and the sky has become orange. I have never seen it look like this in Ahmedabad.

We have just passed a station called Valsad. The train stopped for only two minutes, but even for the short time, there was so much noise. "*Chai! garam, chai!*" one man was calling, "*batata vada! batata vada!*

puri-shaak!, doodh-thanda-doodh!." People were selling and buying food on the platform. We quickly bought some bananas and *chikoos* through the window itself.

- What did Omana see from the window?

____

____

- What are some of the things that are sold at Railway stations?

__________ __________ __________ __________

__________ __________ __________ __________

__________ __________ __________ __________

16 May

I have made some friends. They are Sunil and Ann. They are going to their grandmother's house in Kozhikode. Sunil has given me some story books to read.

A little while ago, I went to brush my teeth, but there was no water in the bathroom. Somebody said that it will only be filled at the next big station.

For the teacher: Gandhidham, Ahmedabad and Valsad are in Gujarat. Kozhikode is in Kerala. Show these states to the children on the map to help them realise what a long journey it is.

- Why do you think there was no water in the bathroom of the train? Discuss.
- Imagine that you are going on a long train journey. What are the things that you will take with you to help pass the time?
- Can you recognise who are these people shown in the picture? What work do they do? Discuss.

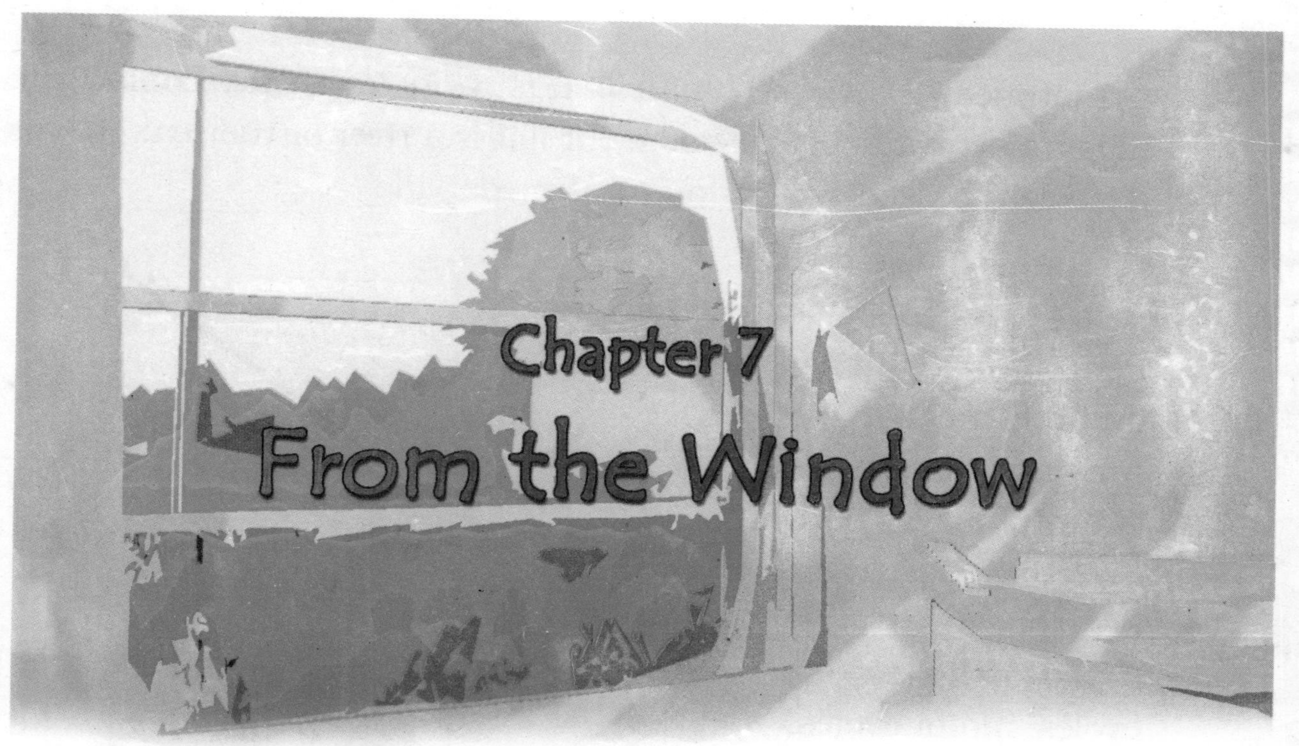

Chapter 7
From the Window

17 May

It is morning now. Last night I went to sleep early. It was too dark to see anything outside. When the train stopped early this morning, I woke up. It was Madgaon. That was written on the board at the platform. *Appa* said that we were going through the state of Goa.

We got off at the station and had some hot tea and filled our water bottles. The train started again. I find it difficult to describe the scene outside. It is so beautiful. It is green everywhere – fields with red soil and green crops, hills covered with trees.

Sometimes, I can see small ponds, and far away, behind the hills, more water. I can't make out if it is a river or the sea. The air is cooler, and not so dry as in Ahmedabad.

The train passed a 'level crossing'. People are waiting on both the sides of the crossing for the train to pass. There are buses full of people, cars, trucks, autorickshaws, cycles, motor cycles, scooters and even tongas and bullock-carts with people and goods in them. Some people do not switch off the engines of their vehicle even while waiting at the level crossing. There is a lot of smoke and noise. I see some people going under the bars of the level crossing. How dangerous this is!

At times our train crosses another train. Unni and I tried to count the carriages in one such train, but both the trains were going so fast. We always got confused.

- What was the difference in the scene that Omana saw from the train on the first day and on the second day?

____

____

____

- Omana saw many kinds of vehicles at the level-crossing. Which of them run on diesel or petrol?

____

____

- Why was there so much smoke and noise from the vehicles at the level crossing?

____

____

- What can we do to reduce noise of the vehicle and save petrol and diesel? Discuss.

____

____

Sometimes people cross the tracks even when the crossing is closed. What do you feel about this?

17 May

Later, I was sitting near the window with my eyes closed. Suddenly the sound of the moving train changed – khud, khud, khud... I opened my eyes. Guess what I saw? Our train was crossing a very big river, on a very long bridge! As it was crossing the bridge it sounded very different. The wheels rattled as there was no ground, only the tracks, and the water down below. When I first looked down, I felt giddy. It was really quite scary! The river down below was full of water and had some boats. I could also see some fishermen

on the banks. I waved at them, but I did not know if they could see me.

Alongside our bridge, there was another bridge for buses and cars. This was built differently from ours. I think going over our bridge was more adventurous!

- Have you seen any bridges? Where?

  ____

- Have you ever crossed a bridge? Where?

  ____

- What was the bridge built over?

  ____

- What did you see below the bridge?

  ____

- Find out why bridges are made.

  ____

  ____

17 May

The last few hours have been so exciting. After breakfast, I climbed on to the upper berth to read my comics. It was bright and sunny outside. Suddenly, everything became dark. It also felt a little cold inside. I was afraid. Then the lights in the train came on. But outside, it was very dark. Somebody said, "We have entered a tunnel. This goes right through the mountain." The tunnel seemed to go on and on. And then, just as suddenly, we were in daylight again. Outside it was sunny, bright and green. The train had crossed the tunnel. *Appa* explained that we were on the other side of the mountain. Since then, we have passed through four smaller tunnels. Now I am enjoying going through the tunnels.

- Have you ever been through a tunnel? How did you feel?

  ____

- The route from Goa to Kerala has a total of 2000 bridges and 92 tunnels! Why do you think there are so many bridges and tunnels?

  ____

  ____

◎ Imagine and draw in your notebook what Omana saw under the bridge when her train crossed it?

◎ Imagine, if on the way there had been no tunnels and bridges, how would Omana's train have crossed the moutains and rivers?

17 May

Now it is afternoon. For lunch we had *idli-vada* that we bought from Udipi station. We also bought some bananas. These were very small and very tasty. The scene outside has changed again. Now we can see many coconut trees, and green fields everywhere. *Amma* says that these are paddy fields. The houses and villages look very different. People's clothes are also different from what we see in Ahmedabad. Most people are wearing white or cream-coloured dhotis and sarees. Many people who were with us from Ahmedabad have got off. People have also got on to the train from different stations.

Sunil's family is getting off at Kozhikode, which comes at around 6 O'clock. We have exchanged addresses and plan to meet in Ahmedabad. You will also like Sunil and Ann.

◎ Which languages do you speak at home?

◎ On the way from Gujarat to Kerala Omana's train went through several states of our country. Find out and list which states it crossed.

◎ Did you ever have coconut water? How did you find it? Discuss.

◎ Draw a coconut tree and discuss in the class about it.

- Find out in which states these languages are spoken?

Language	Where it is spoken (State)
Malayalam	______________
Konkani	______________
Marathi	______________
Gujarati	______________
Kannada	______________

17 May

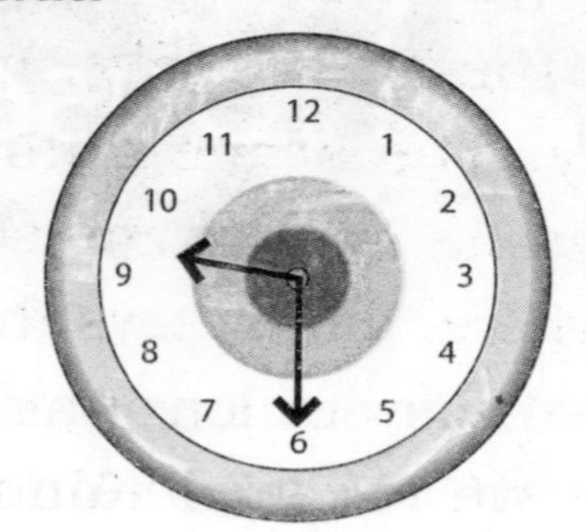

Now it is night. We have also started packing up. The train will reach Kottayam in about three hours. That is where we have to get off.

Tonight we will go to *Valiyamma's* house. Tomorrow, we will take the bus that will take us to *Ammumma's* village. We all are quite tired. After all, we have been on the train for two days. What a long journey it has been! We had a lot of fun. I will put my diary away now. I will write again after we reach *Ammumma's* house.

- What do you call them?

Your mother's sister	______________
Your mother's mother	______________
Your father's sister	______________
Your father's mother	______________

For the teacher: Help the children to find out about the different states, languages, clothes, food and landforms. Mother's elder sister is called *Valiyamma* and mother's mother is *Ammumma* in Malayalam.

Chapter 8

Reaching Grandmother's House

17 May Night

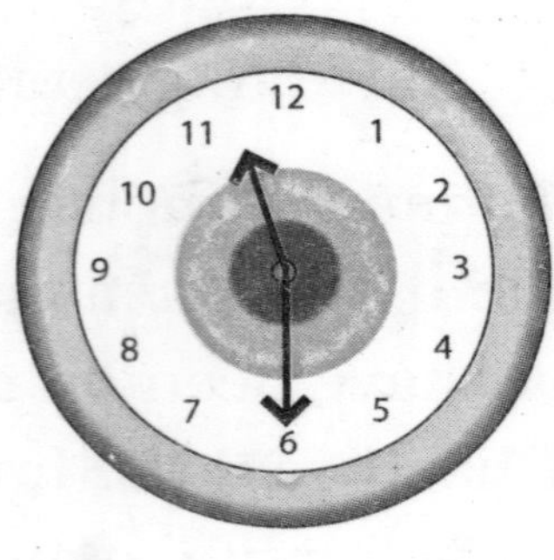

After our long train journey we reached Kottayam in the night. *Valiyamma's* house was not far from the station and we had to take two auto-rickshaws to get there. By then I was very sleepy and did not even wait to eat anything. I took a bath and slept. I thought, I had just fallen asleep when *Amma* woke me up again. We got ready, took our luggage and went to the bus stand. *Valiyamma's* family also came with us. We were ten people, and had a lot of luggage too!

The bus conductor came and *Appa* bought tickets for all of us. We managed to get seats. As it went along, the bus got very crowded. People were sharing the seats. We also had to share our seats.

After a long ride, the bus reached the last stop, I was happy to get off. My legs were stiff. I could hardly stand.

I thought that we had finally reached *Ammumma's* village. But no! Our travel had not ended yet. The bus had dropped us by the water side. "Look", *Amma* pointed across the water. "That is where we have to go." "But how will we get there?" I wondered.

Just then I saw a boat coming. "There is the ferry," *Amma* said. Immediately a big crowd of people started getting off – school children, men, women, all with their own packets and luggage. *Amma* explained that the ferry was used by people to cross the water and reach the other side.

As soon as the ferry got empty, the big rush started from our side. Everyone had to pay the fare before getting on. Very soon the ferry was full. It started off again.

I managed to get a place to stand along the railing. I saw the rippling of the still water as the ferry moved. It was moving smoothly on the water. There were rows of coconut trees on the banks of the river. As we moved swiftly, I could see people, fishing, washing, bathing and working along the banks.

Just before the sun disappeared into the water, the ferry reached the island and stopped. It was time for us to get off. At last, we reached *Ammumma's* place. What a long and interesting journey it has been!

- Omana travelled by different kinds of transport after she got down from the train. Can you remember what these were?

- On which vehicles have you travelled?

- Which ride did you enjoy the most? Why?

- Omana left Ahmedabad on 16 May. How many hours did it take for her to reach *Ammumma's* place?

- Have you ever been on a long journey? Where did you go?

  - Name the different kinds of transport that you used during the journey.

For the teacher: In many parts of Kerala the ferry and other kind of boats are commonly used to travel from one place to another. Discuss why these are used. You can also ask children about boat rides that they have taken.

- How long did your journey take?

____

- Omana's *Appa* bought tickets for the train and the bus. Can you think of other means of transport for which we need to buy tickets?

____

____

- Sometimes we need to buy tickets to enter a place. Can you think of such places?

____

- Look at this picture of a railway ticket. Find the following information on the ticket and circle them with different colours and discuss.

- The train number _______________
- The date of the start of the journey _______________
- The berth and the coach numbers _______________
- The fare (the cost of the ticket) _______________
- The distance (in kms) _______________

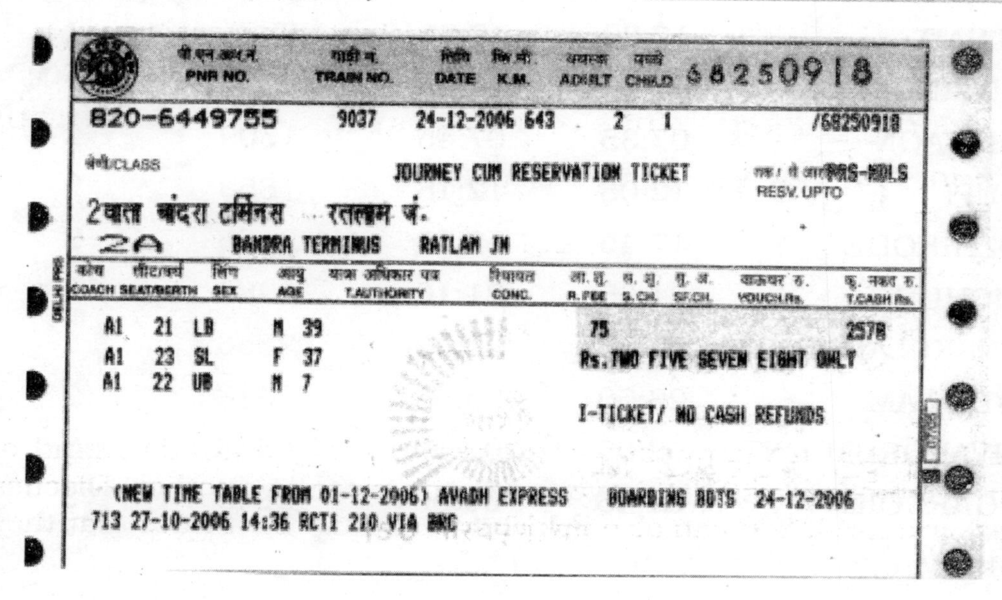

PNR NO. | TRAIN NO. | DATE | K.M. | ADULT | CHILD 68250918

820-6449755 9037 24-12-2006 643 2 1 /68250918

CLASS JOURNEY CUM RESERVATION TICKET RESV. UPTO PRS-NDLS

2वाता बांदरा टर्मिनस रतलाम जं.

2A BANDRA TERMINUS RATLAM JN

COACH	SEAT/BERTH		SEX	AGE	T.AUTHORITY	CONC.	R.FEE	S.CH.	SF.CH.	VOUCH.Rs.	T.CASH Rs.
A1	21	LB	M	39			75				2578
A1	23	SL	F	37							
A1	22	UB	M	7							

Rs.TWO FIVE SEVEN EIGHT ONLY

I-TICKET/ NO CASH REFUNDS

(NEW TIME TABLE FROM 01-12-2006) AVADH EXPRESS BOARDING BDTS 24-12-2006

713 27-10-2006 14:36 RCT1 210 VIA BRC

Write what other information you can find out from the ticket.

- ____________________
- ____________________
- ____________________

A railway time-table gives details about the route of every train – the stations along the route, what time the train will reach and leave each station, the distance covered, etc. We can buy a railway time-table from a railway station.

Some portions of the time-table for the route of the train on which Omana travelled are given. Look carefully at it and answer the following questions.

6335 NAGARCOIL EXPRESS

S.No	Station Name	Arrival Time	Departure Time	Distance (Kilometre)	Day
1.	GANDHIDHAM	–	05:15	0	1
2.	AHMEDABAD	11:30	11:50	301	1
3.	VADODARA	14:03	14:10	401	1
4.	SURAT	16:15	16:20	530	1
5.	VALSAD	17:23	17:25	598	1
6.	BHIWANDI ROAD	21:10	21:12	772	1
7.	MADGAON	07:35	07:45	1509	2
8.	UDUPI	12:06	12:18	1858	2
9.	KOZHIKODE	17:45	17:50	2165	2
10.	TRICHUR	21:05	21:10	2280	2
11.	ERNAKULAM TOWN	22:35	22:40	2356	2
12.	KOTTAYAM	23:50	23:55	2418	2
13.	TRIVANDRUM CNTL	03:05	03:10	2578	3
14.	NAGARCOIL	04:45	00:00	2649	3

- Circle the names of all the stations in the table that are mentioned in Omana's diary.
- From which station did the train start?

  ___

- How many minutes did the train stop at Ahmedabad station?

  ___

- On which day of the journey did the train reach Madgaon?

  ___

- Sunil and Ann got off at Kozhikode station. Omana got off at Kottayam station. How many hours does the train take to reach Kottayam from Kozhikode?

  ___

- What is the distance that the train travelled over the whole route?

  ___

- How many kilometres did Omana travel by train?

  ___

- Would you like to keep a diary? Take a notebook or a diary. Every day for a week, write about what you did. Also write your thoughts and feelings. Share your diary with your friends.

For the teacher: Try to bring a railway time-table to the class. Help the children to learn how to read the time-table. You can use the time-table to devise many interesting activities to teach geography, mathematics, etc.

Chapter 9

Changing Families

Here are some pictures of families. These are the families of Nimmi, Tsering and Nazli. Let us look at these pictures, talk about what we see and discuss.

A New Arrival!

There is great excitement in Nimmi's family. She has a new baby sister.

Look at the pictures and write

- Who were the members of Nimmi's family before the arrival of her baby sister?

  Nimmi, Father, Mother, Grandmother, Grandfather

- How many members are there in Nimmi's family now?

  6 members

Let us talk

- How do you think the lives of Nimmi's family members have changed after the arrival of the new baby? For example –
  - How will Nimmi spend her day now?
  - What new work will her mother do now?
  - There will be a change in the daily work of Nimmi's father, grandmother and uncle with the arrival of the new baby. Can you tell how?

For the teacher: Give an opportunity to each child to share his or her experiences.

- Has a small brother or sister been born in your home or in any house in your neighbourhood?
  - How does it feel to have a new baby at home?
  - How have things changed at home with the new baby?
- Find out all about the youngest child in your home or in the home of a relative. Then write –
  - When was the baby born?

    ____

  - Is the baby a boy or a girl?

    ____

  - How are you related to him or her?

    ____

  - Where was the baby born?

    ____

  - Who does the baby look like?

    ____

  - What is the colour of his or her hair?

    ____

  - What is the colour of his or her eyes?

    ____

  - Does the baby have any teeth?

    ____

  - What is the baby's length?

    ____

- How many hours a day does the baby sleep?

  ___

- What different sounds does the baby make?

  ___

- Who does the baby stay with most of the time?

  ___

- Stick a photograph of the baby or draw a picture in your notebook.

New Place

Tsering's father received a letter from his office. The letter said that he was being promoted and would have to move to another city.

When Tsering's father showed the letter to his family, how do you think the different members would have felt?

- What will change in Tsering's family after his father's transfer? For example –
  - Who from Tsering's family will live with his father at the new place? Which school will Tsering go to now? Will he have new friends?
  - Has anybody in your family moved to a new place because of work?
  - What do you feel about this change?
- Is there anyone in your class or school who has come to your school from another place? If so, talk to him or her.
  - Where has she or he come from?
  - What was his or her old school like?
  - What does he or she find different here?
  - Does he or she like the change?

It's a Wedding!

There is great joy in Nazli's home today. Her elder cousin brother is getting married.

Let us talk

Do you think that there will be any change in Nazli's family after this wedding? What will change?

- Do you think there will be changes in the home from where the new bride has come? What kind of changes?

- Talk to your mother and aunts in the family. Ask them about where they lived before they got married.
- Who were the members in their families then?
- Has anybody in your family been married recently? Who?

- Talk to your classmates and write all about what happens during weddings in their families.

  ____

  - What kind of special food is cooked?

  ____

  - What special clothes do the bride and bridegroom wear?

  ____

  - What kinds of songs and dances are performed at weddings?

  ____

What did you see at the wedding that you attended? Draw some pictures in your notebook. Then look at the pictures drawn by your classmates.

We saw changes taking place in the families of Nimmi, Tsering and Nazli because of different reasons.

Write down the reasons for these changes

- In Nimmi's family –

  ____

  ____

- In Tsering's family –

  ____

  ____

- In Nazli's family –

____

____

- There can be many reasons for changes in families. Can you think of some more reasons?

____

____

____

- Talk to three old people – one from your family, one from your friend's family and one from a family in your neighbourhood. Ask them these questions and fill in the table.

Question	**Your family**	**Friend's family**	**Neighbour's family**
• Since how many years has your family been staying here?			
• Where did your family live before coming here?			
• How many members are there in your family today?			
• How many members were there in your family 10 years ago?			

For the teacher: Changes are a part of life. However, children can be deeply affected by changes. It is important to be sensitive about this while discussing this topic.

• What were the reasons for the changes in your family in the last 10 years?			
• How do you feel about all these changes?			

My Family – Yesterday, Today, Tomorrow...

All families change in some way or the other because of different reasons. Has your family changed too?

When your grandmother and grandfather were children like you, was your family just like it is today?

Do you remember the picture of Sitamma's family tree which we saw in Class III?

- You had also drawn a family tree of your own family. Let us again draw the family tree of last year in your notebook.
- Ask your grandmother or grandfather how many members were there in their family when they were your age? Then draw a family tree in your notebook of their family when they were young.
- Can you see yourself, your brother or your sister, your mother or your father, anywhere in this family tree?
- Now draw a family tree of your present family in your notebook.

Can you see yourself anywhere in this family tree? Who are the members of your family today? Where are your grandparents?

Let us talk

Can you tell in what ways the family tree of your grandmother or grandfather in their childhood is different from your family tree today?

Going Back to School

- Upto which class do you want to study?

  ___

- Upto which class have your parents studied?

  ___

- Till which class did your grandmother get a chance to study?

  ___

- At what age did your grandmother get married?

  ___

- Have you heard of a Law that talks about the ages before which girls and boys must not get married?

  ___

  ___

There are many girls who get married before they are 18 years old. Many of them have to even leave school. There are many true stories of girls like Susheela of Ranga Reddy district who are going back to school. She also got the help of the *Panchayat*. The *Panchayat* said that young children should play and study and not be married off. A group of people of Andhra Pradesh holds special camps to help married girls to go back to school. Jangamma and Chitti say, "We would like to study and stand on our own feet."

Find out and write

- Are there any such children in your neighbourhood who had to drop out of school? Do they want to go back to school?

- What are they doing these days?

- Has anybody in your family got married recently? Who?

- What was the age of bride and the groom?

- What kind of dresses they wored?

Bride

Groom

- What kind of dishes were there? Name them.

For the teacher: Teacher can discuss about children who cannot finish school and also the Law on Child Marriage, which has strictly fixed the minimum age for marriage for girls at 18 and for boys at 21 years.

Chapter 10

Hu Tu Tu, Hu Tu Tu

Hu-tu-tu, Hu-tu-tu, Hu-tu-tu, Hu-tu-tu,
Out, out (all the girls on one side shouted loudly).
Hu-tu-tu, Hu-tu-tu, Hu-tu-tu (hold from here)
Hu-tu-tu, Hu-tu-tu (hold from the leg, the leg, the leg – hold her leg).
Hu-tu-tu, Hu-tu-tu (Vasudha, you come here, you hold her from here).
Hey! Make sure that Shyamala's hand does not touch the line.
Hold her hand.
Hu-tu-tu, Hu-tu-tu – Oh! She has touched. She has touched it. –
Out, out, out. All out. Ho, ho, ho
Your team is all out!

What are these girls doing? They are shouting 'out','out','out', it is clear that they are playing a game.

What do you call this game? Chedduguddu, Hu-tu-tu, Choo Kit Kit, Ha-du-du or Kabaddi or something else?

When six girls surrounded Shyamala and caught her, everyone thought that she was 'out'. Somebody caught her legs, and somebody her arms, while one girl caught her by the waist. But Shyamala was not the one to give up. She dragged herself and managed to touch the line in the centre.

When Shyamala touched the line, all the girls of the opposite team were holding her. So all of them got 'out'. But Rosy argued that Shyamala had taken a breath in between, so the team was not 'out'. Shyamala insisted that this was not true. She said that if she had taken a breath, why did the girls keep holding her? There was a big argument. Finally Shyamala won.

For the teacher: Using this game, bring children's attention to this point that we make rules for our lives, the way we do for games, so that things can be done in a proper manner. We may have differences and fights among ourselves, and we do resolve them.

- When you play Kabaddi, how many players do you have in a team?

  ____

- How many players got out when Shyamala touched the line?

  ____

- When you have an arguement or fight during a game, what do you all do to solve the problem?

  ____

  ____

The Game of Kabaddi

So, this is what a game of Kabaddi is like. Pushing and pulling, screaming and shouting, dragging and falling on the ground. It is a rough game, yet it has many rules.

It is lots of fun and lots of exercise. Holding your breath while running and continuously saying Kabaddi-Kabaddi and also trying to touch the players of the opposite team. So many things to do in Kabaddi. You can do this as long as you can hold your breath.

You need to use both your body and mind in this game. You have to use your strength to pull or stop the players. At the same time, you have to think about how to enter the other side. You have to decide whom to touch quickly and come back. If you get caught, then how do you reach the line in the centre?

For the teacher: You can organise a discussion on the topic that in games also, many a times the children experience discrimination on the basis of gender, caste and class.

- **Try to hold your breath and keep saying Kabaddi- Kabaddi. How many times could you say it?**
- **How many times can you say it, while you are playing Kabaddi? Is there any difference?**

Next time when you play Kabaddi, focus your attention on your legs, arms and eyes. You will notice that good coordination is required between eyes, legs and arms.

- Make a picture in your notebook to show how Shyamala managed to get the entire opposing team 'out' in one go.
- What does it mean to be 'out' in games? When does one gets 'out' in Kabaddi?

____

____

- In some games it is very important to touch the player. For example in the game of Kho-Kho, you get 'out' when someone touches you. You also get your turn by someone's touch. Name some games in which it is very important to touch the players?

__________ __________ __________

- In Kabaddi, the entire team was 'out', because Shyamala had touched the line. What are some other games in which, the central line is very important?

__________ __________ __________

- What are the games in which , besides the players, you have to touch some things or colours?

__________ __________ __________

For the teacher: The activity given above in the box should be done only under the teacher's or elder's supervision.

Do you play Kabaddi? Is there a girls' Kabaddi team in your school? Do you think that your grandmother played Kabaddi when she was your age? Ask her.

Do girls in your area play Kabaddi or any other outdoor game? If there are girls who do not play, then what are the reasons for them not playing? Discuss.

Karnam Malleshwari

Have you seen or read about her in the newspapers? Karnam Malleshwari is a weight lifter. She lives in Andhra Pradesh. Her father is a police constable. Malleshwari started lifting weights when she was 12 years old. Now she can lift a weight of 130 kilograms.

Karnam has won 29 medals in international events. Her four sisters also practise weight lifting.

A Story of Three Sisters

Look at this photograph. Don't they look like simple grandmothers? But they are different.

The picture is of the three sisters – Jwala, Leela and Heera. They live in Mumbai. All three of them played Kabaddi, and taught the game to others. Jwala tells, "When we were young, girls were not allowed to play this game. People thought that if girls played such rough games, nobody would marry them." They also said that the girls had to wear boys'

clothes to play Kabaddi. That is why they stopped girls from playing.

The sisters were young when their father died. Their mother and *mamas* (maternal uncles) brought them up. Both uncles used to play Kabaddi and Kho-Kho. They encouraged the three girls to play Kabaddi.

Jwala and Leela talk about their experiences. "Almost fifty years ago when we started to play Kabaddi, girls never got a chance to play this game. Parents did not let them play the game. But we always felt that we should play and my uncles and mother supported us. We three learnt the game and some other girls also joined us. We formed a *Kabaddi Club*, which is active even today."

Remembering Those Days!

Leela and Heera still get very excited when they talk about their matches. They tell how they won some matches which they were about to lose. This was possible because of their strong will. During those matches, some very interesting things happened. Once they had to go to a different town for a big match. Leela tells, "The match had to start at 6.30 in the evening. We went to see a movie from 3 to 6 o'clock. We thought we would be back in time for the match. As soon as the movie started, we noticed some noise and disturbance. It was created by our *mama*, who was looking for us in the hall with a torch. When he found us, he gave a big scolding right there in the cinema hall."

For the teacher: Use these examples to draw children's attention to the reality that many times girls do not get equal opportunities in games. Ask children what they call their 'maternal uncle'.

The sisters had to face many difficulties because of Kabaddi but that did not stop them from having fun. Heera, the youngest sister, became a Kabaddi coach. She wishes that children like you should enjoy and play many games, especially Kabaddi.

- Have you learnt any game from a coach? Which one?

  ____

- Do you know of anyone who has learnt any game from a coach?

  ____

Discuss

- How does a coach teach? How does a coach make a player practice? How hard do you think the players have to work?
- Have you ever thought of making a club for your favourite game?
- Imagine that there are 15 children to play Kho-Kho. They must form two teams with equal numbers (7 each). Then one player will be left. What will you do if this happens? Have you ever become the 'extra person' in the middle? Write about this.
- Every game has some rules. The game is played according to those rules. Let us see what happens if the rules are changed. For example – In cricket, a batsman gets 'out', if the bails fall off the stumps. Imagine if there is a rule that the entire team will be 'out', if all the three stumps fall. Would it be fun?
- Try and play the game with this rule. Similarly, make some rules for other games and play.

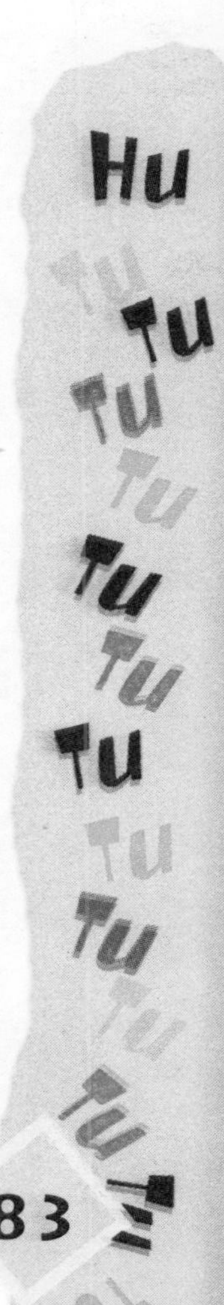

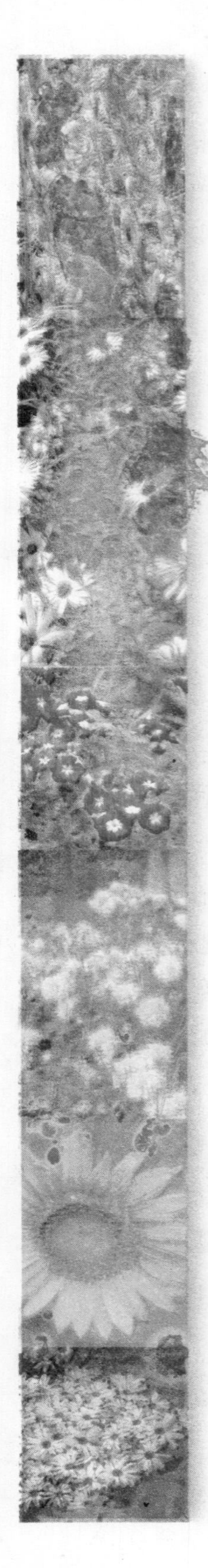

Chapter 11
The Valley of Flowers

In the hills of Uttarakhand there is a place where there are flowers everywhere. This place is called the 'Valley of Flowers'. In some places, one sees red flowers blooming on bushes, while in others one finds white flowers peeping out between the stones. There are wide areas carpeted with the brightest yellow flowers. And suddenly, elsewhere, blue flowers shining like tiny stars between the grass. All this seems like a beautiful dream, doesn't it? Yes, because like a dream these flowers bloom only for a few weeks in the year.

Now close your eyes and imagine that you have reached such a place. How does it feel? Which songs do you feel like singing?

- Have you ever seen so many flowers growing together anywhere? Where?

  ____

- How many differently coloured flowers have you seen?
- Write their colours.

  ________ ________ ________ ________

  ________ ________ ________ ________

Now you were just left counting, weren't you?

Are there any things in your house which have designs of flowers made on them – like clothes, sheets, vases, etc.?

Here is a floral design in the box below.

The design in the picture is called 'Madhubani'. It is a very old form of folk art. Do you know why it is called Madhubani? There is a district in Bihar called Madhubani. Here, during festivals and happy occasions, the walls of the houses and their courtyards are painted with such pictures. These paintings are made out of paste of powdered rice in which colour has been mixed. The colours used in Madhubani painting are very special too. To make them, indigo (*Neel*), turmeric (*Haldi*), colours from flowers and trees, etc., are used. The paintings show human beings, animals, trees, flowers, birds, fish and many other animals.

Draw your own design in your notebook and colour it as well.

Look at the designs made by your friends as well.

For the teacher: Encourage children to locate Uttarakhand on the map.

The World of Flowers

Here are some pictures of flowers. Mark a (✓) on the flowers which you recognise. Write their names too if you know.

- From the pictures given above, and other flowers that you know, give names of two flowers which
  - grow on trees ____________ ____________
  - grow on bushes ____________ ____________

- grow on creepers ______ ______
- grow on water plants ______ ______
- bloom only at night ______ ______
- bloom in the day and close at night ______ ______

- Which flowers can you recognise by their scent, even with your eyes closed? ______ ______
- Which flowers bloom all the year round? ______ ______
- Which flowers bloom only in certain months ? ______ ______

Are there any trees or plants which never have any flowers? Find out and write.

____

Why this?

- Have you ever seen a board like this put up anywhere?
- Do people pluck flowers even when this board is there?
- Why do you think they do this?
- Should they do this?
- What would happen if everybody plucked flowers?

____

Let us look closely

Children who can bring flowers may bring one or two flowers to class. Remember that you must collect only fallen flowers. Do not pluck any flower. Make groups of three or four children and look at one flower carefully –

- What is the colour of the flower?

  ____

- What kind of a scent does it have?

  ____

- What does it look like – a bell, a bowl, a brush or anything else?

  ____

- Do these flowers grow in bunches?

  ____

- How many petals does it have?

  ____

- Are all the petals joined together or separate?

  ____

- Outside the petals, can you see any green leafy structure? How many are there?

  ____

- Inside the petals, in the middle of the flower, can you see some thin structures? Write the colour.

  ____

- When you touch these, do you find a powdery thing on your hands?

____

Blooming buds!

You must have seen buds on the plants. If there are any flower bearing plants growing near your school or home, look carefully at their buds.

- What differences do you find between a flower and a bud?

____

____

- Draw the picture of a bud and its flower in your notebook.
- Can you tell how many days will a bud take to bloom into a flower? Let us try and find out.
  - Choose a bud that is growing on a plant and look at it everyday. Write the name of the plant.

    ____

  - When you first saw this bud, the date was ________. Now when the bud has bloomed into a flower, the date is ______. How many days did the bud take to become a flower?

    ____

  - Ask your friends the names of the different flowers that they have seen. How much time did it take their buds to become flowers?
  - Also observe how many days it took for the same flower to dry up.

So many uses!

Flowers are even eaten!

What are the different ways we use flowers in our daily life? Do you know that flowers can be eaten as well? Many flowers are cooked as vegetables.

In Uttar Pradesh, Firoza and Nilima enjoy eating a vegetable made of *kachnar* flowers.

In Kerala, Yamini wants her mother to cook her a vegetable made of banana flowers.

Mamta and Omar who are from Maharashtra love *pakoras* made of *sahjan* flowers.

- Are flowers cooked in your home as a dry vegetable, a gravy dish or as a *chutney*? Find out which flowers are used for these.

Flowers in medicines!

Flowers are used to make many medicines as well.

- Find out names of any two flowers which are used for making medicines?

  ______________________________ ______________________________

How is rose water used in your house? Is it used as medicine, sweets, *lassi* or something else? Find out and tell others.

Colours from flowers

Colours are made from many flowers like marigolds, zenia, etc. These colours can also be used to dye cloth.

- Find out and write the names of some more flowers that are used for making colours.

____

____

- Can you think of a colour of which there is no flower?

____

- Write the names of such flowers which are used to make scents.

____

____

____

You may have heard of some of Granny's old recipes which use flowers. Here is a recipe for which rose water is used.

GRANNY'S RECIPE

Mix equal part of rose water and glycerine. Fill this in a bottle. Add a few drops of lemon juice. In winters use this mixture on your skin. Your skin will not crack or dry.

Have you experienced the smell on opening a small bottle of *Itr*? Do you know – even a small bottle of *Itr* is made from lots and lots of flowers?

The Kannauj district in Uttar Pradesh is famous for *Itr*. Truckloads of flowers are brought from neighbouring areas for this purpose.*Itr*, rose water, *Kewra* water are prepared from flowers here. Thousands of people in Kannauj are engaged in this work.

For the teacher: Encourage children to locate Uttar Pradesh, Kerala and Maharashtra on the Map. Discuss with children that *Itr* is a pure extract of flowers.

Other Uses

- Have you ever read or heard any songs about flowers? Let us sing this song –

  "अच्छी मालन, मेरे बन्ने का बना ला सेहरा,
  बागे जन्नत गई मालन मेरी फूलों के लिए,
  फूल न मिलें तो कलियों का बना ला सेहरा।"

  "Good gardener, make for my Banna a garland of flowers;
  She went looking for flowers in the garden in heaven;
  Make a garland of flower-buds if there are no flowers..."

Talk about it

- Do you know when such songs are sung?
- Do you or anybody else at home know other such songs?

  Collect songs, poems, etc., on flowers. Write them down and put them up in the classroom.

- Are any special flowers used on certain occasions/festivals by your elders? Make a list of different occasions and the flowers used at each.

Occasion/Festivals	Name of flower

For the teacher: *Banna* - bridegroom. Ask children what they call bridegroom in their area.

Of course, if there are so many uses of flowers, then we need lots and lots of flowers. Flowers are grown in many places. Imagine fields full of flowers extending for miles together! How beautiful!

Let us know some more

Have you ever seen anyone selling flowers anywhere? If there are any flower-sellers nearby ask them these questions and write –

- What are the different flowers that they sell? Ask them the names of three flowers.

  __________ __________ __________

- Where do they bring these flowers from?

  ____

- Why do people buy flowers?

  ____

  ____

- In what forms do flower-sellers sell their flowers? Look at these picture. Tick against those forms that you have seen.

Any other form that you have seen –

- Some flowers are used in different forms – like rose and marigold are used in garlands and as loose petals too.
  - Find out the prices of these different forms.

    One flower ____________

    One garland ____________

    One bouquet ____________
  - Has the flower-seller learnt to make bouquets or a net of flowers from anybody? From whom?

    ____

    ____
  - Would they like the other members of their family to do this work? Why?

    ____

    ____

    ____

Let us do this activity

You could do this in groups of five or six each.

- Collect flowers that have fallen from trees or plants and bring them to the class.
- Spread these flowers neatly between the sheets of an old newspaper.
- Make sure that the flowers do not touch each other.
- Now put a heavy object on the newspaper. Leave it pressed for ten to fifteen days at one place.
- After this, take out all the flowers very carefully and prepare a scrap book. You can take a used notebook or old newspapers for this.
- You can also use these dried flowers to make pretty cards.

Write a poem in your own words on your favourite flower.

____

____

____

____

For the teacher: Encourage children to observe flowers closely. The children should be helped to group flowers based on easily observable characteristics - like number of petals, colours, whether in bunches or not, etc.

Chapter 12
Changing Times

My name is Chetandas. Many years ago I used to teach children like you. These days I spend my time by writing about the days when I was young. I would love to share some of these with you.

A Big Move

I remember the time when I was nine years old. It must have been over sixty years ago. That was when we lived in Dera Gazikhan. Today this place is in Pakistan. At that time, there were a lot of problems all around us. I could not understand what was happening. One day *Baba* told us

For the teacher: Before starting this lesson, you can talk to the children about how India got freedom from the British rule, and also about the partition. Show them India and Pakistan on the map.

that we had to leave our village and move to another place. I was sad to leave my house and my village. That was where I had all my friends. All of us – *Baba*, *Amma*, my younger brothers and sisters and I took a train to come here, near Delhi. Like us, many people from our area also moved. People were saying that our country was being divided into two – India and Pakistan. Many people from India went to Pakistan, just like we had moved to India. For some time we all stayed in a camp. We lived in big tents that were put up in a huge ground.

A New Home

One day *Baba* told us that we had been given some land in Sohna village. He said that we could build our house there. I was very happy. *Baba* and *Amma* worked hard to make the house. We children also helped. *Baba* dug the soil, and we quickly filled the pans and passed them on to *Amma*. Gudiya and *Amma* mixed husk in it. *Baba* put up the walls.

We brought cow dung from nearby houses. *Amma* mixed it with the mud. She coated the floor with this mixture, just like she used to do in our old house. *Amma* used to say that this would keep the insects away.

Then, it was the turn for the roof to be made. *Baba* made a frame by joining strips of wood and fixed it on the four walls. We put branches of *neem* and *keekar* trees on the frame, so that termites would not harm the wood. *Amma* put old gunny bags on this and covered them with mud.

Most of the houses around our house were made like ours. A few were different. But I liked my house the best. It was just like our old house.

Find out and Write

- Talk to any one of your grandparents or any other elderly person. Find out, when she or he was eight-nine years old –
  - Where did she or he live? Name that place.

    ____
  - From what material was her or his house made?

    ____
  - Did they have a toilet in their house? If no, where was it?

    ____
  - In which part of the house was food cooked?

    ____
  - A lot of mud was used when Chetandas' house was made. Why?

    ____

For the teacher: Sohna village is in Haryana. Ask the children to locate Haryana on the map. Point out that when Chetandas' parents built their house, most of the material they used were locally available. Discuss about locally available material and their uses.

A Changing House

Time passed quickly. I finished my studies and got a job. *Amma-Baba* wanted me to get married. I thought that before I got married we should repair our house and build one more room. In those days, people in cities were using cement. They said that this made the houses stronger. We also thought we would use cement. We used iron and cement for making the roof of the new room.

In those days unbaked bricks were also available in the market. We made the walls with them. The use of bricks was useful – we did not need to coat the wall every week. Once a year we would whitewash the walls. We also built a small kitchen in the courtyard. The kitchen had a mud *chulha* and place to keep the vessels.

Then I got married, and my wife Suman came to our new house. To cook, Suman used to sit on the floor in the kitchen. We all used to sit on mats in the kitchen and eat together. It was a happy time!

People used to go out to the field for their toilet in those days. Some of the houses had a separate place for this. We also made a small toilet with unbaked bricks behind the house.

- Chetandas tells that people from the basti used to come to clean the toilets and take away the waste. They were not allowed to enter the house.
  - The people who used the toilets did not clean them. Discuss.
  - Is there a toilet in your house? Who cleans it?

More Changes

My two sons and a daughter were born in that house. Time passed. The children completed their studies. Fifteen years ago, our daughter Simi got married and moved to Palwal. When Raju was to get married, we felt that we should get the house ready for the new bride.

By then, everyone was using baked bricks. We also used them for the walls and put a lintel for the roof. We used marble chips and cement for a strong and fancy floor. In the toilet we put pipes to take away the waste. The kitchen was made bigger. Now, Raju s wife does not use the clay *chulha*. She stands while cooking on the gas stove.

For the teacher: Ask the children what they think about the cleaning of toilets by others. Do they know of places where this is still done?

Seeing New Things

My younger son Montu moved to Delhi when he got a job there. Now he stays there with his family. Suman and I stay with Montu for some months in a year, and with Raju in Sohna for the rest of the time. On the way to Delhi from Sohna, we go through Gurgaon. So many big high-rise buildings have come up there!

A few years ago Raju renovated the toilet and the bathroom. He used coloured tiles in his bathroom. Imagine, spending so much money for a place to have a bath!

I am now seventy years old. In all these years, I have seen so many changes, even in my own house. I don t know where my grandchildren will want to live and how their house will be! I wonder what the houses are like in Dera Gazikhan today. And how about all my friends – where will they be?

- What material have been used in making your house?

____

____

- Find out the material from which your friend s house is made? Is there any difference? Write about it.

____

____

- What kind of house do you think Chetandas grandchildren will live in?

____

____

- Where would you like to live when you grow up? What kind of house would you like?

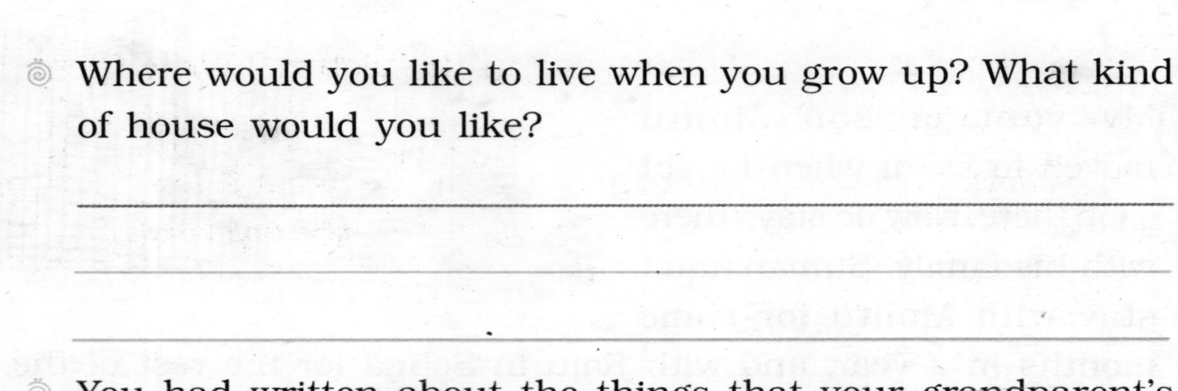

- You had written about the things that your grandparent's house was made of. Has some of the same kind of material been used in your house? Name them.

- People are given names according to the work they do. For example, a person who works with wood is called a carpenter.
  - In your place, what do you call a person who works with wood?

Now, look at the picture and fill in the table.

What kind of work is being done by different people here?

What tools are they shown using in the picture? Write them in the given table.

Work	Tool	What is the person called
1. ________	________	________
2. ________	________	________
3. ________	________	________
4. ________	________	________

Do you know people who do these type of work? Talk to them and find out about their work. Discuss it with your friends.

- With your teacher or someone from home, go to a place where a building is being constructed. Talk to the people working there and find out answers to these questions.
  - What is being built there?

    ____

    ____

  - How many people are working there?

    ____

    ____

  - What kind of work are they doing?

    ____

    ____

  - How many men and women are there?

    ____

    ____

For the teacher: If there is a construction site near by, you should take the children to visit it. Let them interact with the people working there.

- Are any children working there? What are they doing?

- How much money do these people get paid daily? Ask any three different people about this.

- Where do these people live?

- What are the materials being used for making the building?

- Try and guess how many trucks of bricks and bags of cement will be used for making the building.

- How do the materials reach the building site? (By truck, handcart, any other vehicle) List them.

- Find out the price of

  One bag of cement ____________

  One brick ____________

  One truck of sand ____________

For the teacher: Invite some of the people from the construction site to your school to talk to the students about their work and tools.

- Ask a few other questions and write their answers.
  - ______________________________
  - ______________________________

- Over the sixty years, different materials were used at different times in Chetandas' house. List these in the correct order.

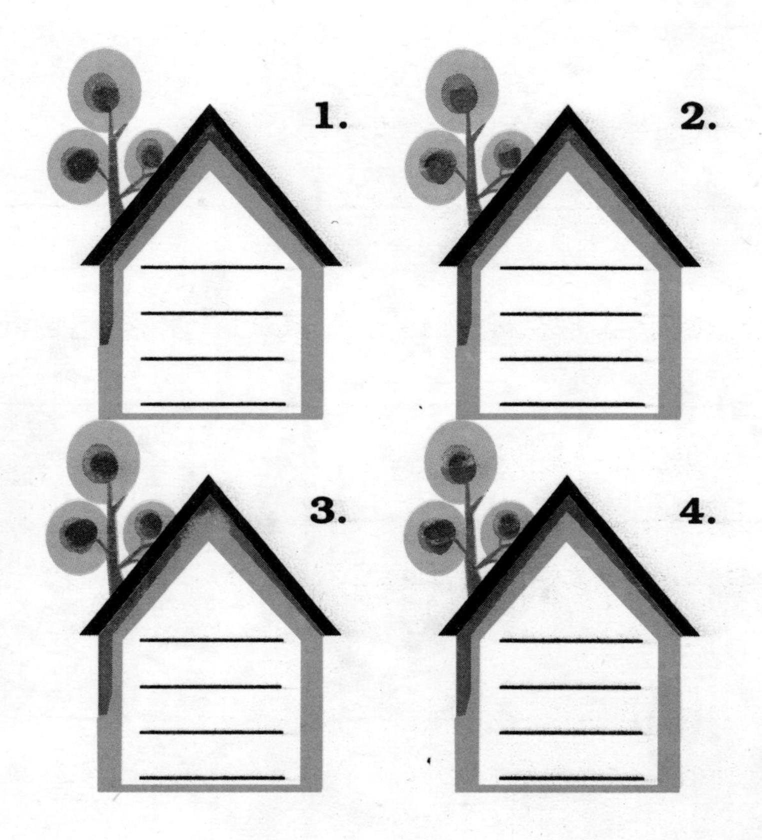

Let us make houses

- Divide the children in the class into 3-4 groups. Let each group make a model of a different house. For this you can use mud, wood, paper, pieces of cloth, shoe-boxes, match boxes and colours.
- Place all the houses so as to construct a neighbourhood colony.

Chapter 13

A River's Tale

Look carefully at the picture of the river. Read the words given below. Use these words to make a story. Give a title to your story also.

Boat, flowing water, blue, fish, water-plants, river, foul smell, big ship, oil, river banks, factories, washing clothes, animals, other work, change, city.

Look at the pictures and answer the following questions:

- What is the colour of the river where it begins?

- At some places, there are many fish in the river, at others there are only a few and at some places there are dead fish. What could be the reason for this? Discuss.
- What can be seen in the river before it reaches the village?

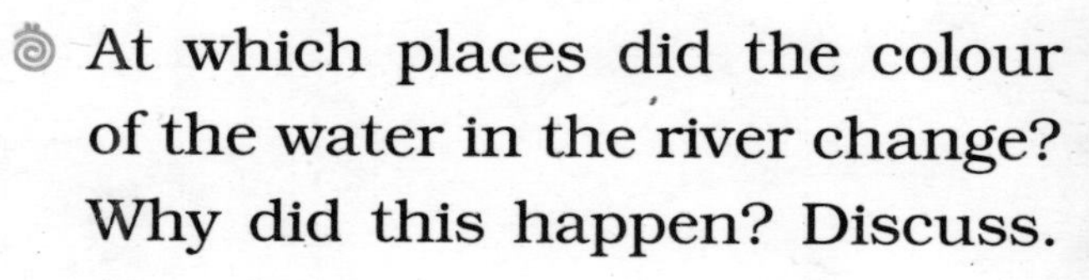

- At which places did the colour of the water in the river change? Why did this happen? Discuss.
- Which of the places shown in the picture would you like to live in? Why?
- Would you like to change any of the things that you see in the picture? Why and how?
- What could be done to keep rivers clean? Discuss.

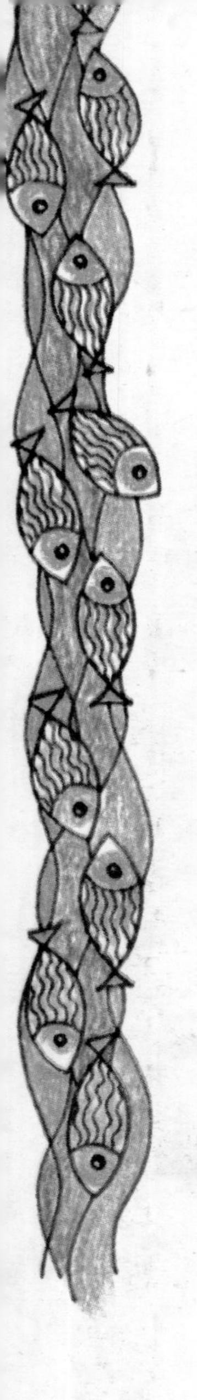

- If you wanted to drink some water, from which part of the river would you like to drink? Why?

____

____

- In the last part of the picture the river flows into the sea. Have you ever seen the sea? Where? In a movie, or somewhere else?

____

- Have you ever been near a river or sea? When?

____

- Show with your hands, how the waves in the sea move.

____

- Is the water from the sea drinkable? Why?

____

- Do you think that there would be changes taking place in a river, pond or stream at different times of the year? What kind of changes would these be? Discuss.

- Will there be the same amount of water in the ponds or rivers during the rainy season and in summer?

- Is there a pond, river or lake near your town or city? Find out–
  - Are there any changes in the water during summers, the rainy season and in winters?
  - What are the different kinds of water animals found there?
  - What kind of trees and plants grow around it?
  - What are the kinds of birds that come there?
  - Have you ever seen or read about floods? Where?
  - What happens when there is a flood?
  - Have you seen dirty water in a river or pond? Where?
  - How would you know if the water is dirty? If the water looks clean, can you be sure that it is alright to drink that water? Discuss.

How does Water become Dirty?

You saw in the pictures that as the river flowed through or near many villages, towns and cities the water changed. The people used the river water for many different things such as washing clothes, bathing animals and cleaning utensils. Many of these activities made the water dirty. The water in the river kept changing as it flowed through various places. Water in ponds and lakes can also become dirty due to similar reasons.

From where do you get your drinking water? A river or a lake? Do you think that like the river in the picture your river or lake can also be affected?

Try this

- For this activity you will need to bring certain things from your home. You will find most of these in the kitchen.
- 5 or 6 glasses or bottles.
- Salt, sugar, cooking soda, *haldi*, flour and *dal* (about half a teaspoon each).
- Lemon Juice, soap water, *sherbet*, oil (one spoonful each).

What will you do?

Fill about half of each bottle or glass with water. Make sure that all have the same amount of water. Now, one by one, put each of the things in the water. For example – *haldi* in the first glass, oil in the second glass, soda in the third glass until you have one thing in each glass. Mix each thing in the water and see what happens. Write your observations in the table.

What did you observe? Put (✓) mark in the right places.

Things	Dissolved (mixed) in water	Did not dissolve in water	Colour of water changes	Colour of water does not change
Sugar				
Salt				
Lemon juice				
Haldi				
Soap water				
Flour				
Dal				
Sherbet				
Cooking soda				
Oil (Mustard, *Til* or any other)				

Now on the basis of your observations tell –

- Do all things dissolve in water?
- Does the colour of the water always change?
- Did oil dissolve in water? How can you say whether it has dissolved or not?

Colour of the water may not change even after some things are dissolved in it. Would you say that these are absent in water?

Imagine how it would be if things like sugar, salt, lemon juice, *sherbet*, etc., could not dissolve in water!

Imagine how it would be if things like stones, chalk, plastic and garbage would dissolve in water!

There are many things that dissolve easily in water. Some of these can be very harmful for our body. Hence, it is important

that we clean water before drinking it. One of the best ways to do this is to boil the water. If for some reason this cannot be done, can you think of some other ways to clean water?

- How is drinking water cleaned in your house?
- Find out the many different ways of cleaning water at home.
- Draw pictures showing any two ways of cleaning the water.

Chapter 14

Basva's Farm

I am Basva. My father is a farmer. We live in Belvanika village in Karnataka. It is the month of July. Like every year, *Appa*, my father, is preparing the field to sow the onion crop. There are so many things to be done at this time. To help him I too go to the field with *Appa*. In the last few days, *Appa* has been using the *Khunti* (an iron rod) to dig the soil, loosen it and make it soft.

Find out

- In Basva's area an implement called *Khunti* is used to loosen the soil. What is this kind of implement called in your area? Draw it and discuss.

For the teacher: This lesson talks about the process of cultivating an onion crop. You can use this as an example to encourage children to find out and describe the process for growing some crops that are common in their area.

- Find out from a farmer or some elders in your family, what kinds of crops are grown in your area.

Sowing the Seeds

This year also my father will sow onion seeds in the field. The bullocks will pull the *Kurige* and *Appa* will walk behind them,

sprinkling the seeds. I would also like to do this, just like my *Appa*. But *Appa* says that it is necessary to drop the right amount of seeds at a regular distance. This is not so easy to do. He says that I may drop too many seeds at one place. I must wait till I am a little older to be able to do this properly.

- What other ways could be used to plough the fields instead of animals. Discuss.

The Sprouts Appear

It is now twenty days since the seeds were sown. The onion plants have started to sprout. Along with onion plants, weeds have also come up. Weeds grow in fields and gardens, without being planted. *Appa* says that we must remove the weeds so that they do not take up all the water and fertilisers. If there are too many weeds, then the onion plants will not be healthy. *Amma*, Uncle and I, we all help *Appa* to take out the weeds.

Growing Plants

I am happy to see the plants growing. They are tall enough to reach my knees. The leaves have started turning yellow and drying up. This means that the onions are ready to be taken out.

- Draw any crop which you have seen in the field.

Do you know why?

Everyone at home will have to work to take the onions out. It is important that this should be done at the right time. If we are late, the onions will rot in the ground itself and all our hard work will be wasted.

- Basva helps his father in the field. Do you help the elders in your family in their work? What do you help with?

____

____

- Do you enjoy doing that work?

The Onion Crop

Everyone at home is happy. This time the onions are big and healthy. *Amma* and aunty use the *illige* to cut the dried leaves from the top of the onions. The *illige* is sharp and you have to be careful not to cut your fingers. *Appa* and Uncle fill the sacks with onions. *Appa* will take them in a truck to sell in the big market.

Write answers in your notebook

- Why is Basva not able to attend school for some days?
- Are there any fields near your house? What is grown there?

- Basva's *Appa* takes the onions to the market in a truck. Think, how would fruits and vegetables be taken to another place, if there were no proper roads.
- What kind of vehicles are used to carry fruits and vegetables? Draw a picture of one of these vehicles in your notebook.

Find out and write

- Given here are pictures of some implements used by Basva's family. Write the names of the implements. Also write what these are called in your area? For what work are they used?

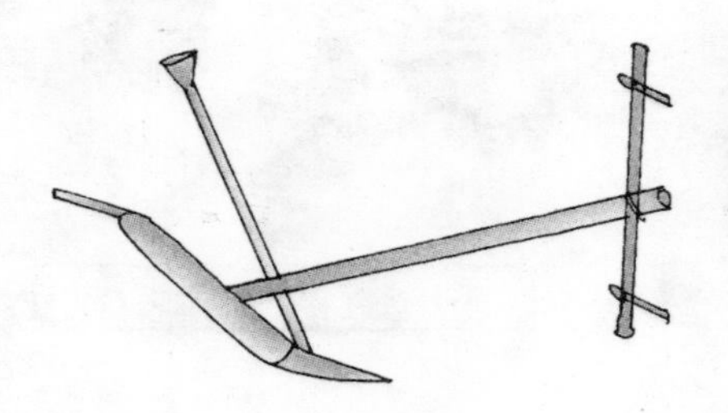

Name (in this chapter) ______________

Name in your area ______________

Work ______________

Name (in this chapter) ______________

Name in your area ______________

Work ______________

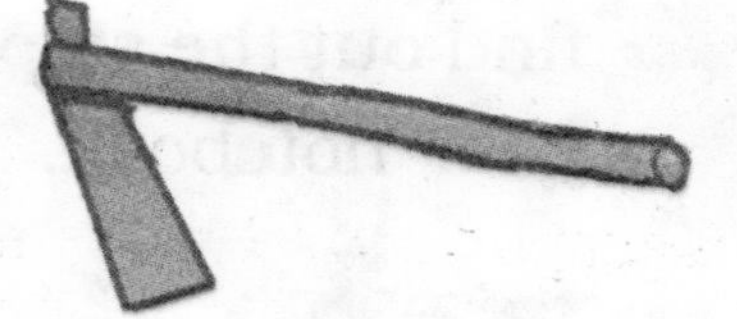

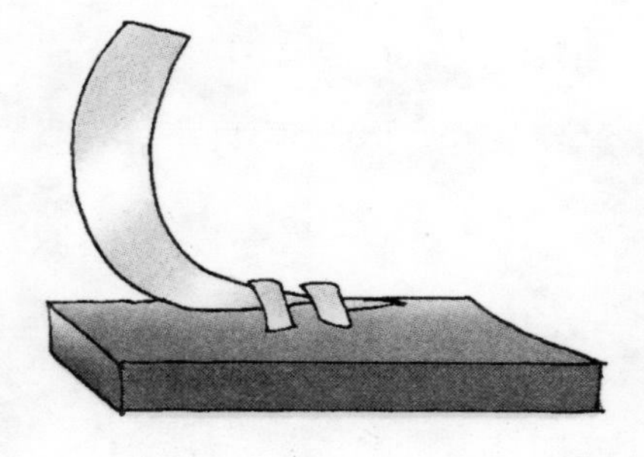

Name (in this chapter) ______________

Name in your area ______________

Work ______________

◎ Many steps are needed to grow crops. Look at the pictures and mark them in the correct order.

◎ Find out about a crop that is grown in your area. Also find out the steps that are part of this work. Draw them in your notebook.

Chapter 15
From Market to Home

Day at night!

My name is Vaishali. My father is a vegetable-seller. My whole family – *Amma*, *Bhaiya*, *Chhotu* and I, help him with his work. Can you guess at what time we begin our work? At 3 o'clock in the morning. When most people are fast asleep, we start our work. Our day's work begins when *Babuji*, *Amma*, *Bhaiya* and I take out the previous day's vegetables from the gunny bags and baskets. This is to prepare for bringing the fresh vegetables from the *mandi*. Sometimes *Chhotu* also helps us.

As we finish doing this and are having some tea, we hear the horn of the tempo. It is time for *Babuji*, *Bhaiya*, *Chachu* (uncle) and some others from our street to leave for the *mandi*.

- Does anyone in your house have to get up very early? What time does he or she get up? Why do they need to get up so early?

____

____

____

Preparing for the Day

While *Babuji* is away, *Amma*, Chhotu and I put the previous day's vegetables on gunny bags, and sprinkle some water on them. By 6.30 a.m. *Babuji* is back from the *mandi* with baskets and sacks full of fresh vegetables. At that time our house looks more like a small vegetable market! There are brinjals, potatoes, tomatoes, okra (*Bhindi*), pumpkin, gourds, chillies and many other vegetables all around. Everybody helps in sorting the vegetables. The vegetables which are not fully ripe and ready to sell are kept aside. We have to sort the vegetables fast, so as to reach the *bazaar* as early as possible.

For the teacher: Discuss the role of vegetable *mandi* with the students.

By 7 o'clock, *Babuji* arranges all the vegetables on the handcart and leaves for the *bazaar*. He says that if he is late, then his regular buyers may buy their vegetables from someone else. As soon as *Babuji* leaves, I quickly get ready as I have to reach school by 7.30 a.m.

In the Bazaar

Chhotu attends school in the afternoon. He rests for a while and goes to the *bazaar* later with food for *Babuji* and *Bhaiya*. He stays with them at the vegetable cart, until it is time for him to go to school. Sometimes he goes back after school to help *Babuji*. *Babuji* tries to see that the previous day's vegetables are sold first.

Let us talk

- *Babuji* sells the previous day's vegetables first. Why do you think he does this?
- Have you seen dried or spoilt vegetables? Where?
- How did you know that the vegetables were spoilt?

As the previous day's vegetables get sold, *Bhaiya* takes out fresh vegetables from the sacks and puts them in the cart. He also keeps sprinkling water on the vegetables so that they do not dry up, especially in summers. *Babuji* and *Bhaiya* return home, after a long day, only around 10 o'clock at night. By then Chhotu and I are asleep. Everyone else sleeps around 11 or 11.30 at night. And at 3 o'clock next morning – only four hours later – our family is up again. Another day has begun!

- Look at the clocks given below. Write what you do, and what Vaishali does, at the time which the clocks are showing.

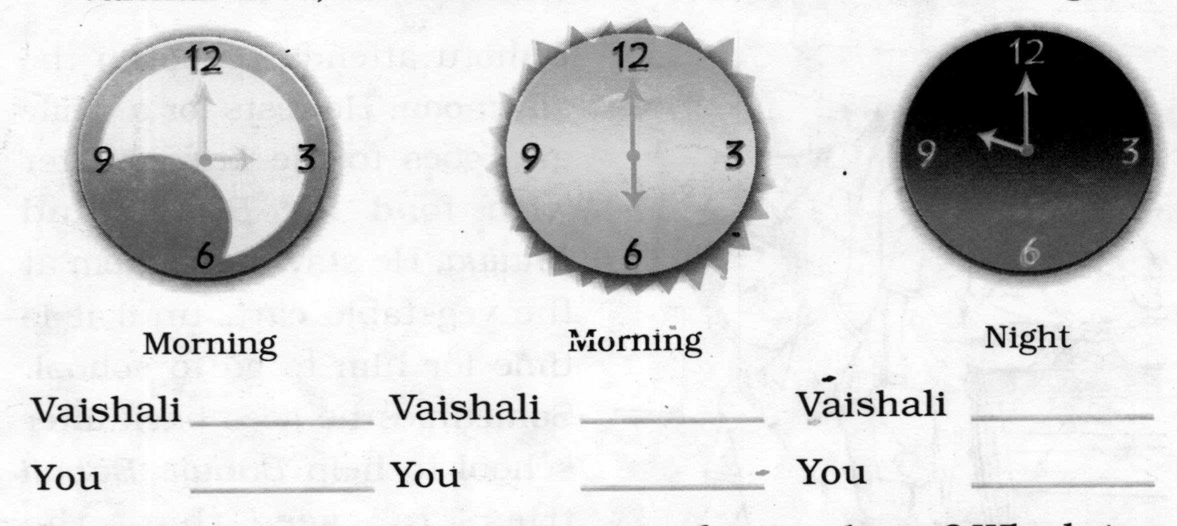

Morning	Morning	Night
Vaishali ________	Vaishali ________	Vaishali ________
You ________	You ________	You ________

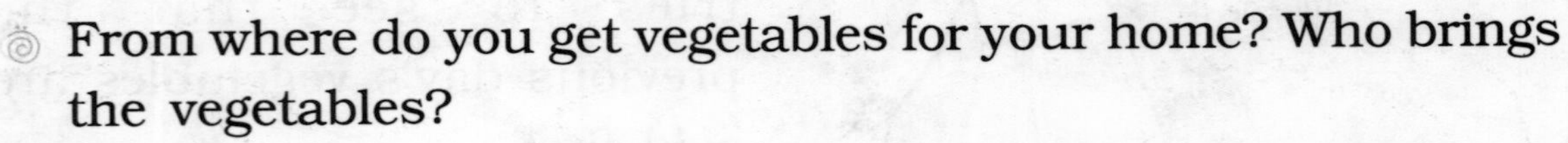

- From where do you get vegetables for your home? Who brings the vegetables?

____

____

Some fun with vegetables

The next time when you get okra (*Bhindi*) at home, look at them carefully. Are all of them the same size?

- Find the longest and the shortest one. Measure them.
- Do all the okra (*Bhindi*) have the same thickness and colour? Cut two okra (*Bhindi*) lengthwise. Do both of them have the same number of seeds? Draw them in your notebook.
- Seema's mother has brought some fruits and vegetables from the market. Can you find them in this picture? Colour them and write their names alongside.

Find out

- Given here is a list of vegetables and fruits. Which of these will spoil earlier, and which will stay for some days? Write the names in the correct column. You can add more names in the list.

Spinach	**Potato**	**Banana**	**Tomato**	**Pear**
Chikoo	**Pineapple**	**Gourd**	**Onion**	**Cabbage**
Cucumber	**Grapes**	**Ginger.**		

Fruits and vegetables that spoil quickly	Fruits and vegetables that can stay for some days
______ ______	______ ______
______ ______	______ ______
______ ______	______ ______
______ ______	______ ______
______ ______	______ ______
______ ______	______ ______

Some of these fruits and vegetables are smooth to touch while some are rough. From the list above, put the names in the correct column.

Smooth	Rough
______ ______	______ ______
______ ______	______ ______
______ ______	______ ______
______ ______	______ ______

- Which vegetable do you find the heaviest to carry? Write its name and draw its picture in your notebook.
- Which is the lightest fruit or vegetable that you have eaten? Write its name and draw the picture in your notebook.
- Write names of three vegetables which do not have seeds.

______________ ______________ ______________

Fill in the table given below. You can add three more names and fill in the table.

	Colour	Length	Weight	Price
Apple			(kilo)	
Banana			(1 dozen)	
Potato			(kilo)	

- Talk with a vegetable-seller in your area. Ask the following questions and make a brief report in the notebook.
  - What is his or her name?
  - How many people are there in his or her house? How many children are there at home?
  - What are the names of the children? How old are they?
  - Who all help in the work o. selling vegetables?

- Who all stay with the vegetable cart or sit in the shop?
- What vegetables do they sell?
- What time do they start work?
- For how many hours in a day do they work?
- Ask them about any three vegetables that they sell.

	Vegetable 1	**Vegetable 2**	**Vegetable 3**
Name of the vegetable			
The price of the vegetable			
Where does it come from?			
How much of the vegetable do they buy at one time?			
In which months does this vegetable usually come?			

Chapter 16

A Busy Month

Balmandir
Bhavnagar, 13 April, 1936

Dear Children,

It is 3 o'clock in the afternoon. There are no clouds in the sky. The sun is burning hot.

The sparrows, doves and sunbirds have started working in pairs as they prepare to make their nests. Some of the birds have already made their nests. In some of the nests, the eggs have hatched. The parent birds are busy feeding the chicks with different kinds of insects and other things.

Dove

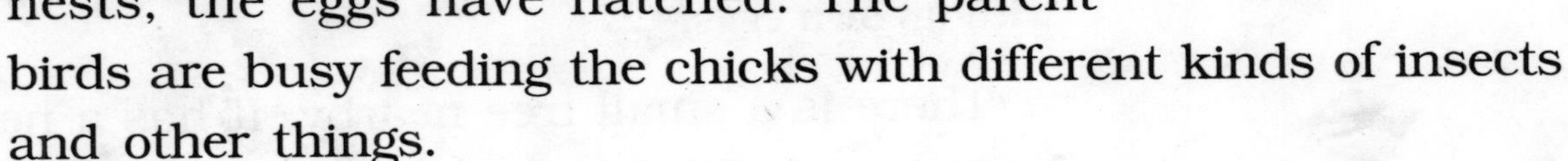

In our courtyard also, there is a baby dove. There is another egg in the nest but it has not hatched yet.

For the teacher: Gijubhai Badheka lived in Gujarat. He wrote many stories for children. In this letter you will read about some of the birds that you see all around. After reading this letter children should be encouraged to observe birds around them. Discuss about them in your class.

Indian Robin

On the way to Gopalbhai's house, there are many stones along the roadside. In the space between these stones, an Indian Robin has laid its eggs. Bachubhai showed it to me. I looked through the binoculars. I saw that the nest was made of grass. On top there were soft twigs, roots, wool, hair and cottonwool. This is how the robin makes its nest. What a soft and cozy home for its chicks! The robin is not like the crow. A crow's nest is made of all kinds of things – even pieces of wire and wood.

Crow

I saw a baby bird in the robin's nest. It was sitting with its beak wide open. The mouth was red from inside. In a little while the robin flew to the nest and put something in the chick's open beak – may be a few small insects. By then it was evening. The robin settled down with its chick.

Koel

Barbet

> You know that the Koel sings sweetly. Do you know that this bird does not make its own nest? It lays its eggs in a crow's nest. The crow hatches them along with its own eggs.

There is a small tree nearby. It has a nest hanging from its branch. Birds are so wonderfully different. The crow builds its nest high up on a tree. The dove makes its nest among the thorns of a cactus plant or a *mehendi* hedge. The sparrow can be found in and around our own house. It makes its nest

Tailor bird

anywhere – on top of a cupboard, behind a mirror, on a ledge. Pigeons also make their nest like this. Often they make nests in old or deserted buildings. The barbet or coppersmith bird can be heard in the summer with its 'tuk, tuk, tuk' call. It makes its nest in a hole, in a tree trunk. And the tailor bird uses its sharp beak to stitch together two leaves on a bush. It lays its eggs in the fold of the leaf that it has made. This is its nest.

Sunbird

The sunbird makes a nest that hangs from the branch of a small tree or a bush. The same evening, we saw a sunbird's nest. Can you guess what its nest is made of ? The nest has hair, grass, thin twigs, dry leaves, cottonwool, bits of tree bark, pieces of cloth rags and even spider's cobwebs.

Weaverbird

When I looked through the binoculars, I could see a chick in the nest. It was sitting near the small opening in the nest. It was waiting for its mother to bring some food. What else can it do – just eat and sleep!

Do you know about the weaver bird? The male weaver bird make beautifully woven nests. The female looks at all the nests and chooses the one that she likes the best and decides in which one to lay her eggs.

All the birds are so busy these days. Making a nest and laying the eggs is only the first step. It is a difficult task to raise the young ones in the nest which had been made with so much effort.

Birds have many enemies – humans and other animals too. Crows and squirrels, cats and rats – all of them wait for a chance to steal the eggs. Many times they even break the nest.

To keep oneself safe from danger, to find food, make a nest, hatch the eggs and raise the chicks safely – all these are tests for every bird.

And see – how the birds still sing with joy and spread their wings and fly freely.

So that is all for now, Salaam
Blessings from your
Gijubhai

- How many years ago did Gijubhai write this letter?

  ____

- Find out how old your grandfather and grandmother were at that time.

  ____

- This letter talks about many different birds. How many of these birds have you seen?

  ____

  ____

- How many other birds have you seen? Which ones?

  ____

  ____

- Have you seen a bird's nest? Where did you see it?

  ____

- Which is your favourite bird? Can you show your friends in the class how it flies, and what sound it makes?
- Guess what this bird is –

> 'A crown on the head and coins on the tail,
> So many shades of blue from top to tail.'
> *Clue: It is our national bird.*

- Do you know of any other bird that makes its nest in a tree trunk like the barbet does?

- If there is a nest inside or around your house, look carefully at it. Remember, do not go too near the nest, and do not touch it. If you do, then the bird will not come to the nest again.

  Observe the nest for some days and note down the following things:

  - Where is the nest made?

  - What is the nest made of?

  - Is the nest ready or are the birds still making it?

  - Can you recognise which bird has made the nest?

  - What things does the bird bring to the nest?

  - Is there any bird sitting in the nest?

- Do you think there are any eggs in the nest?

  ____

- Can you hear any sound like 'chee chee' from the nest?

  ____

- If there are chicks in the nest, what do the parent birds bring for them to eat?

  ____

- How many times in one hour do the birds come to the nest?

  ____

- After how many days did the chicks leave the nest?

  ____

- Make a picture of the nest in your notebook.

- You have seen how birds use many different things to make their nests. Use some of these things and make a nest. Make a small paper bird to put in your nest.

Birds use the nest only to lay their eggs. After the eggs have hatched and the chicks have grown, they leave the nest. Imagine, how it would be if we also had to leave our homes as soon as we learnt how to walk and talk!

After they leave their nest, different kinds of birds live in different places – some on trees, some near or on water, and some on land.

Other animals also have different places where they live – on land, under the ground, in water, on trees.

Let us have some fun

- Make three groups in the class. Each child must draw a picture of an animal and colour it. They should then cut each picture out.

- Children in one group will take the cut-outs of the pictures of animals that live on land. They should then draw soil, grass and some trees on a chart paper. Stick the pictures of the land animals at the correct places on the chart.
- The second group will take the cut-outs of the pictures of animals that live in water. They should then colour a chart paper blue to show water. Then also draw water-plants, stones etc. They should then stick the pictures of the animals that live in water on the chart.
- The third group will take the cut-outs of the pictures of animals that live on trees. One child in the group will draw a big tree on a chart paper and colour it. Then all the children in the group must stick their cut-outs of the pictures on the chart paper of their group.
- Put up all the three charts in your class and discuss about them.

Bird Feet – Different Kind for Different Needs

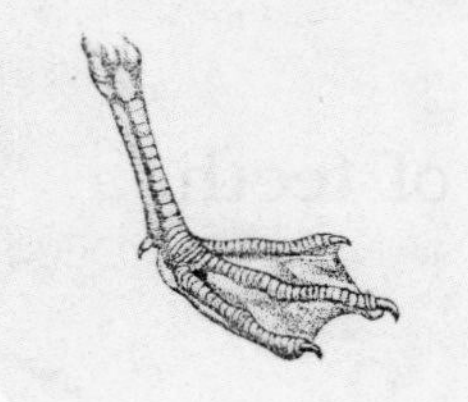

To swim in water

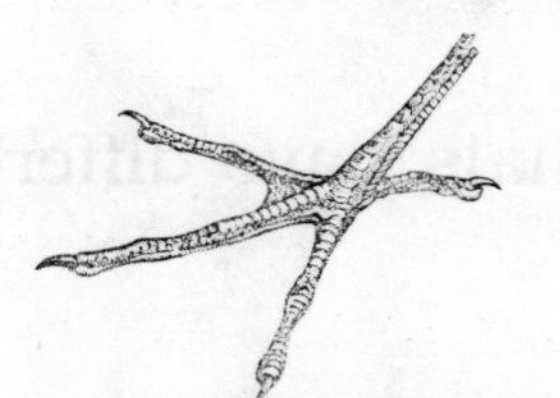

To hold the tree branches

To catch the prey (what it hunts)

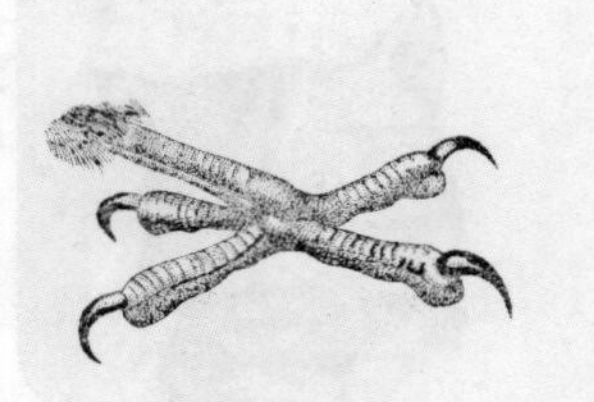

To climb the tree

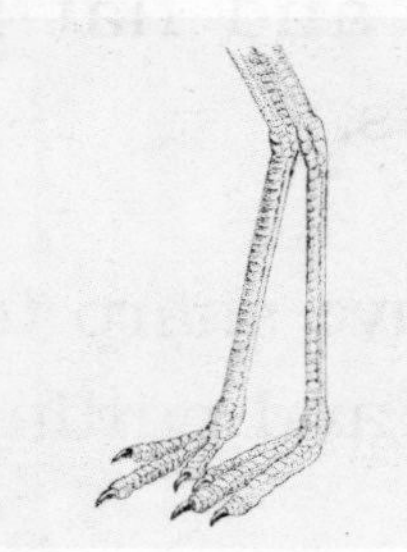

To walk on the land

Bird Beaks – According to the Food

To tear and eat meat

To make holes in wood and tree trunks

To suck nectar from flowers

To find insects and worms from mud and shallow water

To break and crush seeds

To cut and eat many kinds of food

Animal Teeth

You have seen that animals have different types of teeth.

Cows have short front teeth for snipping grass. The teeth on the sides are large and flat for chewing the grass.

Cats have sharp teeth for tearing and cutting meat.

Snakes have sharp curved teeth, but they do not chew their prey. Snakes always swallow their food whole.

Squirrel's front teeth keep growing throughout their life. They have to keep gnawing on things to keep their teeth from becoming too long.

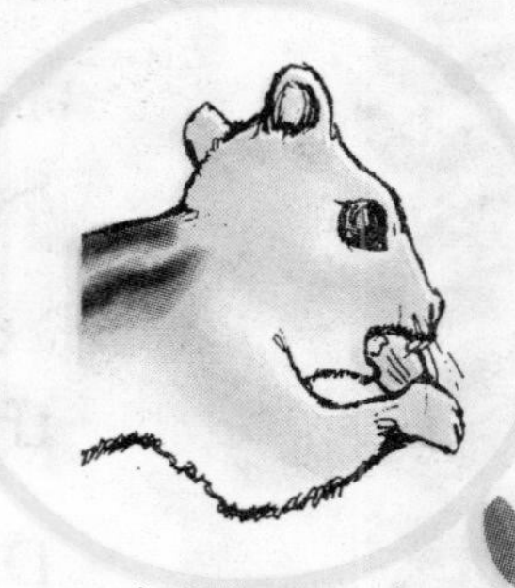

Find out about Your Own Teeth and Write

- Your age:
- How many teeth do you have?
- Have any of your teeth fallen or broken? How many?
- How many new teeth do you have?
- How many of your milk teeth have fallen, but no new teeth have come in their place?

Find out more about teeth

Look at your friend's teeth. Are there different kinds of teeth? Draw one front tooth and one back tooth in your notebook. Can you see any difference between these teeth?

Imagine

- If you did not have front teeth (both top and bottom) how would you eat a guava? Act and show how.
- You have your front teeth, but no teeth at the back. Someone gives you a *roti.* Show how would you eat it.
- You do not have any teeth in your mouth. What kind of things would you be able to eat?
- Draw a picture in your notebook – How would you look if you had no teeth?
- Find out from old people who do not have teeth – what are the kind of things that they can not eat?

Chapter 17
Nandita in Mumbai

I came to Mumbai a month ago. Since we came, mother has been admitted in the hospital. We had to come to Mumbai for her treatment.

The Big City – Mumbai!

I have slowly got used to the city. I still remember the day when mother and I got off the train at the Mumbai station. It was so crowded! I quickly caught hold of mother's hand. I was thinking about how *Mama* would find us in the crowd. Just then, I heard someone calling loudly from behind, "Nandita, Nandita." I turned back, and there was *Mama*.

We left the station and were soon on our way to *Mama's* house. But, again, it

For the teacher: Mother's brother is called *Mama* in Hindi. Ask children what do they call mother's brother in their family?

was so crowded everywhere. There were many huts lined all along the narrow street. We went through the street to reach *Mama's* house. *Mama*, *Mami*, their two daughters and a son – all live in one room. Now, I too live here with them. It is here that we sit, sleep, cook and wash – all in one room.

My house in the village also has only one room, but we have separate places for cooking and for bathing. We also have a courtyard outside.

Water, Water

Mami, Seema and I get up at 4 o'clock every morning and go to the public-tap to fill water. Oh! You won't believe how many fights there are for water. If we are just a little late, then we are not able to fill water for the day. There is no tap in our house in the village too. The pond in the village has water. It takes twenty minutes to walk to it. In summer, sometimes, the water in the

For the teacher: Mother's brother's wife is called *mami* in Hindi. Ask children what do they call her in their family?

pond dries up. Then we have to walk for almost one hour to the river to get water. But in the village, there were no fights for water.

In the street where *Mama* lives, there is a toilet at one end. Everyone in the street uses that toilet. It is always very dirty and smells so bad. At first, it used to make me want to vomit. At times, there is no water. We have to take water with us. Now I am getting used to all this. In the village, people go to the open places or fields for toilet. The men and women go to different places.

- Why did Nandita have to bring her mother from the village to Mumbai?

____

____

- Nandita used to feel like vomiting when at first she had to use the toilet where *Mama* lived. Why?

____

____

____

- In what ways did Nandita find her *Mama's* house to be different from her house in the village?

___

___

___

- What differences did Nandita find between getting water from the public tap and in the village?

___

___

- Was there electricity at the place where Nandita's *Mama* lived? Guess.

___

___

Learning New Things

Everyday I go to the hospital by bus to see my mother. At first, I was too scared to get into such crowded buses. I was not at all used to it. I was afraid. But now, it is not like that. I know how to stand in line, how much to pay for the ticket, where to get down.

Where we stay, there is a tall building nearby. My *Mami* works in seven houses there. She washes utensils and cleans the houses. One day I went there with her. When

I first saw the building, I thought that it was one big house. But I found that there were many houses, one on top of another. I was wondering how I would climb so many stairs, but there was a lift to take people up and down. It was like a big iron cage with fan and light and even a bell. So many of us got into the lift. Somebody pressed the button and lift went up quickly. To tell you the truth, I was very scared in the beginning.

Let us talk

- Do you know anyone who was admitted to a hospital?
  - For how many days was he or she in the hospital?
  - Did you visit the person in the hospital?
  - Who was looking after the patient at the hospital?
- Have you ever seen a tall building? Where?
- How many floors did the building have?
- How many floors did you climb?

Another House

Mami took me first to Babloo's house. His house was on the twelfth floor. What a big house! So many rooms – one to sit in, one to eat in, one to sleep in, and one to cook in. Their toilet was also in the house! It took *Mami* a lot of time to clean Babloo's house, but she could work easily. There was a tap in the kitchen and water flowed from it. Babloo put a bucket under the tap to fill water for his bath. Then he sat down to watch TV. So much water was wasted – I did not like it. I went and closed the tap.

Babloo's house had big glass windows. *Mami* told me to look down from the window. I could see *Mama's* street and the houses, but I could not make out which was his house. From up there, everything below looked like small toys. I was quite afraid to look down from such a height.

When Nandita first came to Mumbai, what were the things that she was afraid to do?

___

___

For the teacher: The lesson describes some differences between where Nandita's *Mama* lives and the houses in the high-rise buildings. Encourage children to think more about such differences and the possible reasons for these.

- What were the differences between the houses where *Mama* lived and the houses in the high-rise buildings?

Houses in area where *Mama* lived	**Houses in a high-rise building**

- Discuss why there were differences.

Tell about yourself

- Draw a circle around the kind of house you live in. Is it like the house of –

Nandita **Mama** **Babloo** **Any other kind**

- Where does the water come from in your house?
- Is there an electricity connection in your house? How many hours in a day do you get electricity?
- Which is the nearest hospital in the area where you live?

How far are these from your house?

	Minutes to walk to	**In Kilometres**
Bus stop		
School		
Market		
Post Office		
Hospital		

Draw pictures in your notebook of the different kind of houses in your area.

A New Worry

Mama had said that he would take me around to see Mumbai. The children around here talk a lot about Chowpatti. They say that big film stars also come there. May be when I go there, I might see a film star!

These days, *Mama* is so worried – I cannot ask him to take me to Chowpatti. Last week some people had come with a notice that everyone should move out of this place. They say a big hotel will be built there. *Mama* was saying that this is the third time in the last ten years that he got such notices. People who live here have been given another place to make their houses. But it is very far away – another corner of the city. There is no drinking water, no electricity. I don't even know if any bus goes there. How will *Mama* reach his work place from so far? How much money will he have to spend, and how much time also. And *Mami*, will she get some other work there! If *Mama* moves to a new place, how will I be able to visit my mother? Mother is not even completely well as yet!

For the teacher: Like Nandita's *Mama*, people sometimes have to vacate their houses and move to another place. Discuss in the class some reasons for this. Also discuss how such changes can affect the whole family.

Write in your notebook

- Why does *Mama* have to change his house?
- Have you ever moved from your house? If yes, why did you have to move?
- Do people in your family have to go far for their work? Where do they go? How far do they have to go?

Discuss

- Is it right that *Mama* and others have to move because a hotel is going to be built there?
- Who will benefit from this?
- Who will face difficulties?
- Do you know of any people who have faced problems similar to Nandita's *Mama*? Talk about it in class.

Draw a picture of house of your choice and colour it.

Chapter 18
Too Much Water, Too Little Water

What to Drink?

Nallamada, Andhra Pradesh

Suguna was reading her book, when she heard someone at the door. She saw that there was a visitor from the city. *Appa* welcomed the guest. He told Selva to bring a cold drink for him. The guest said, "I do not take cold drinks. I will just have a glass of water."

Appa said, "These days we are not getting water that is fit for drinking. It does not even look clean. It would be better if you do not drink this water. We do not have a choice, so we drink it."

Discuss

- How can unclean or dirty water harm our body?
- Have you ever got dirty or unclean water in your area? What was the reason for this?
- Do you know anyone who has fallen sick because of such water? Talk about this.
- When the guest came to Suguna's house, they offered him a cold drink, because they thought he should not drink such water. What do you think Suguna's family must be doing for their own drinking water?
- The guest said he did not take cold drinks. Why do you think he said this?

Water Games

Bazaar Gaon, Maharashtra

There was a big water park near Bazaar Gaon. One day Rohan and Reena went with their parents to the water park. There were many water-fountains. Reena said, "Look Rohan, there are so many rides in the water." "And look at all these big ponds," Rohan said. Splash! Splash! Splash! Both turned around. They saw a long thick water hose going zoom, zoom, zoom.

Children were sliding down a big tall slide and landing in water with a loud splash. Rohan got into a swing high above – whoosh!, Within a second, he had landed in the water. Reena gave a shriek of surprise!

Just then they heard a lot of noise and loud voices from outside the park. Everyone ran towards the main gate. There was a crowd of people, carrying empty buckets and pots. A small child carrying an empty bottle was clinging to his mother. Rohan's mother went to one of the women in the crowd. "What is the matter?" She asked.

The woman replied angrily, "You ask what is the matter? Our wells have no water. We get our water only when the tanker comes once a week. Today, even that has not come. And here, there is so much water everywhere – just for you all to play and enjoy. Tell me, what should we do?"

Read and Write

- Have you ever faced a shortage of water in your house? When?

____

- What did you do then?

____

- Have you ever played in water? Where and when?

  ____

- Are there times when you are not allowed to play in water? What are the reasons for this?
  - ______________________________
  - ______________________________

- Have you seen wastage of water in your area? Discuss.

  ____

- The water park had a lot of water to play in but the nearby village people did not have water even to drink. Think about it and discuss.

- If you go to a water park, find out from where the water comes to the park.

Can We Drink This?

Cuffe Parade, Mumbai

The lift stopped at the 26th floor. Deepak loves going in the lift. Today was a holiday in school. Deepak had gone with his mother to Raziya Madam's house. His mother worked there. The house was quiet and cool, and shining clean. Raziya was reading a newspaper. She smiled when she saw Deepak. "Is it a holiday today?" she asked. She switched on the TV and Deepak was soon lost in the world of cartoons.

Raziya called out, "Pushpa, it says in the newspaper that the gutter water has got mixed with the water in the drinking water pipes, in this area. It says that many people are sick

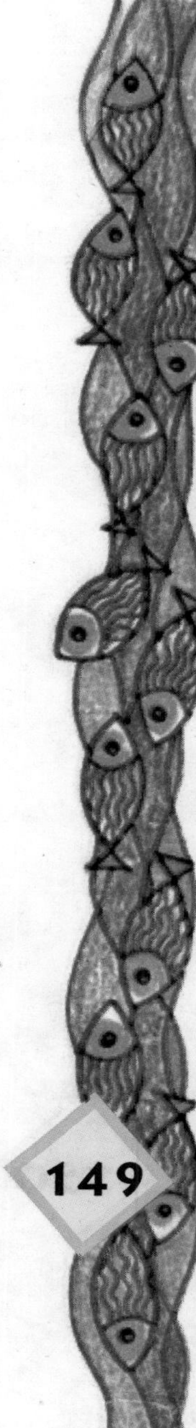

with diarrhoea and vomiting because of this. Why don't you throw away the water that was filled yesterday? Put some fresh water to boil, for drinking. Also take home some boiled water for your family." Deepak was happy to hear this. He thought, "At least today I will not have to stand in a queue for hours to get water for our house. It is a real holiday for me!"

Write in your notebook

- Why was Raziya worried when she read the newspaper?
- Raziya asked that all the water that was filled the previous day should be thrown. Could this water have been used for something else? What kind of things?
- In what way did she plan to clean the water?
- Do you know of different ways to clean the water? Describe them.
- Suppose, Raziya had not read the news and everyone had drunk the water without boiling it, what could have happened?

Discuss

- Where Deepak lives, everyone has to stand in a queue to fill water from the common public tap. In Raziya's house, water comes all day in the tap. Why is this?
- Raziya read news about the water in the newspaper. Have you read any news about water in the newspapers? What kind of news?

Do and Discuss

- Look through the newspapers of the last one month. Look for all news-items related to water. Cut them out. Stick all the cuttings together on a big paper to make a big collage. Talk about what you have collected. Discuss in the class.

Have you ever suffered from diarrhoea and vomiting? How did you feel? When we have diarrhoea and vomiting, we lose a lot of water from our body. This can be dangerous, if we do not take care. It is important that we make up for the water that we lose from our body. We should drink a lot of water when this happens. We should also mix some salt and sugar in the water.

For this, mix one teaspoon sugar and a pinch of salt in one glass of boiled and cooled water. Taste it to make sure that there is not too much salt. The water should not taste more salty than our tears.

When a person has diarrhoea and vomiting, the water must be sipped slowly by them. Light food must be taken. Babies should continue to take their mother's milk as this is good for them. It is also necessary to take some medicines – they can also be home-made remedies. If the diarrhoea does not stop, it is important to get the advise of a doctor.

Water Survey in School

Make three groups of students in your class.

- One group will find out about the arrangements for drinking water in the school.

- The second group will find out about the arrangements for toilets in the school.
- The third group will find out about illnesses affecting children in the class.

The questions given below will help the groups to collect information.

Group 1

Observe and Note –

- Put a (✓) in right box or boxes
  - Where does the water in your school come from?

    Tap ☐ Tank ☐ Handpump ☐ Any other ☐
  - In your school, from where do you take water to drink?

    Tap ☐ Tank ☐ Handpump ☐ Any other ☐
- If there is no tap, *matka* or handpump, then how do you get drinking water?

  ____
- Is there water in all the taps or handpumps?

  ____
- Is there any tap which is leaking or dripping?

  ____
- Are all the *matkas* filled with water and are they covered?

  ____
- Are the *matkas* and other water containers cleaned regularly?

  ____
- How is water made safe for drinking?

  ____

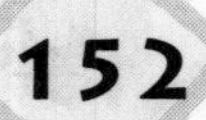

- Is there a long-handled ladle to take water from the *matka* or container? How many ladles are there per container?

____

- Is the place around the drinking water–taps or *matkas* cleaned regularly?

____

Think and Discuss

- Why do the drinking water places get dirty?
- What can we do to keep these places clean?

Find out and Write in your notebook

- How often (once a day, once in two days, etc.) are the containers or *matkas* and ladles cleaned? Who cleans them?
- How many children are there in your school? How many taps, *matkas* or handpumps are there? Are these sufficient for children?
- Who cleans the places near the water?
- Where does the water that is spilt go?

Group 2

Observe and Note –

- Put (✓) in the box and write wherever it is required –
  - What are the toilet arrangements in your school?

    Built toilet ☐ Open area ☐
- How many toilets are there?

____

- Are there separate toilets for girls and boys? ☐ yes ☐ no
- Is there water in the toilets? ☐ yes ☐ no
- Where does the water come from?
  - the tap ☐ yes ☐ no
  - filled containers ☐ yes ☐ no
  - has to be brought from home ☐ yes ☐ no
- Is there water for washing hands near the toilet? ☐ yes ☐ no
- Do you wash your hands after using the toilet? ☐ yes ☐ no
- Is there any tap that is leaking or dripping? ☐ yes ☐ no
- Are the toilets kept clean? ☐ yes ☐ no

Find out and write

- How many boys and girls are there in your school?

  Girls ☐ Boys ☐
- How many toilets are there for girls, and how many for boys?

  Girls ☐ Boys ☐
- If there are no taps, who brings the water for the toilet? From where does the water have to be brought?

  ____
- Who keeps the place clean?

  ____

Talk about it

- What can be done to keep the toilets clean?
- What can each of us do for this?
- Have you seen toilets at bus stands or railway stations? How are they different from the toilets at home?

Group 3

Talk with the children in your class and fill in the table given below. In the last few months, how many children in the class have suffered from any of these? Write the names of the children in the correct columns.

S. No.	Diarrhoea, loose motions	Vomiting	Loose motion and vomiting	Yellow urine, yellow (pale) skin and eyes, mild fever	Stomach ache
1.					
2.					
3.					
4.					
5.					

Discuss with your teacher what you have found out from your survey. Now make a report with your findings and suggestions. Read your report in the assembly. Put it up on the notice board.

For the teacher: The table lists common symptoms that children may know about. If these are caused by cholera, then you can discuss them with reference to this. It is not important that children should know the names of all the diseases.

Children show the Way

Too little water, or no water... this was nothing new for the people in the Holgundi area of Karnataka. The wells would have some water only in rainy days. In the past three years, there was not even enough rain. Everything had dried up there. There was no water for drinking, for growing crops or for animals. People had to leave their village and go to nearby towns for some work. Children had to leave school to go with the elders.

The village *panchayat* was worried. All the members discussed what could be done. This *panchayat* had some special members – children. The children's panchayat was called *Bhima Sangh*.

"Has our village always had water shortage?" the children asked the elders. "No, it was not so before," replied village people. Some of the elders recalled that up on the hill, there used to be a water tank. The tank would fill with water when it rained. There used to be fish in the tank and greenery around it. Those days, even the village wells and the pond used to have enough water. On hearing this, the *Bhima Sangh* decided that they would first look for that tank.

The tank was on the hill. They found that the tank was full of mud and stones now. How could water fill? The tank had many cracks. How could the water remain in the tank? There were no trees and grass – how could there be greenery?

The children said, "We must clean the tank and make the area green again." For this, it was important to first understand how things had been before and why they had changed now. This would help them to plan for solving the water problem. And that too not only for one year, but for the years ahead.

For the teacher: Encourage children to locate Karnataka on the map of India.

The panchayat took help from some experts. Together, they made a plan and together they worked for it.

The tank was first properly cleaned. The cracks were repaired. Grass and trees were planted all around the tank. As the tank was on a hill, a lot of rain water used to flow down the slopes. With this water, soil also would flow away. So the children made a small dam on the slope, to stop the water and soil.

Then everybody waited for the rains to come. When it rained, the tank filled up with the water. The children put some fish in the tank. They kept guard to make sure that nobody stole the fish or harmed the plants. One monsoon went by, then another. Things got better every year. The tank filled a little more, the plants grew, the fish multiplied. After two or three years, the tank remained full of water even after the rains had stopped. The wells and ponds in the village had water again. There was greenery once again. The people did not have to leave their village for work.

The hard work of *Bhima Sangh* had shown results. The children had shown the way! Those children are now grown up. But the *Bhima Sangh* continues, and every year more children are proud to become its members and work together; to always lead the way.

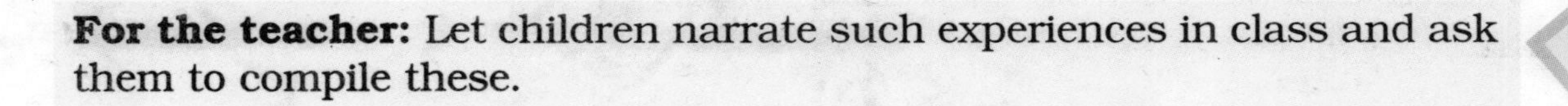

For the teacher: Let children narrate such experiences in class and ask them to compile these.

Abdul in the Garden

It was a holiday. Abdul [illegible]ing his *Abbu* in the garden. *Abbu* was clearing the dried leaves and grass from the vegetable beds. Abdul started to pull out the grass from one of the beds. He found that it was not easy to pull out even the small grass. His hands became red by the effort. In trying to pull out grass, Abdul knocked down a stick that was supporting the pea plant (climber). The delicate stem of the pea plant broke. *Abbu* said, "Why are you pulling the grass? The roots of the grass are strong. You will have to dig them out." Abdul carefully dug out the plant. He then saw that the roots of the grass plant were longer and much more spread out than the part of the plant above the ground.

- The stick which was stuck in the ground fell very easily. It was difficult to pull out a small grass. Why?
- Do all plants have roots?
- Look at some plants and trees around you. Imagine how deep and spread out the roots of these are.

- After three days, Abdul saw that one broken part of the pea plant had dried. Guess which part would have dried up? Why?

Abbu remembered that he had to send some radish (*mooli*) home. He started to pull the radish out of the soil. Abdul wondered whether these were also roots. Only a few radish were pulled when there was suddenly a strong wind and rain. Both of them picked up the radish and ran. They had just reached home when a branch of the neem tree in the courtyard broke and fell. In fact, *Abbu* was lucky to have missed by only a few inches. Despite the strong wind the tree remained firm on the ground. They both sat down to have tea with *Ammi*. *Abbu* said to Abdul, "The plants were getting dry. Now that it has rained, we will not have to water the plants. We can now sit and play *ludo*."

- Why do you think the neem tree did not fall despite the strong wind?
- On putting water in the soil where the plants are growing, the droping leaves become fresh again. How?
- What do you feel, do all plants need water?
- Which of the plants around you need regular watering?

________________________ ________________________

- What will happen, if nobody gives water to these plants?
- Abdul realised that he never watered the huge neem tree. "Where did it get its water from?" he thought. Which of the plants around you do not need watering. Where do they get water from? Make two guesses.

________________________ ________________________

- Abdul wondered whether radish was a root. Why did he think so?

____

____

- Look at the pictures below and find out which of these vegetables are roots.

 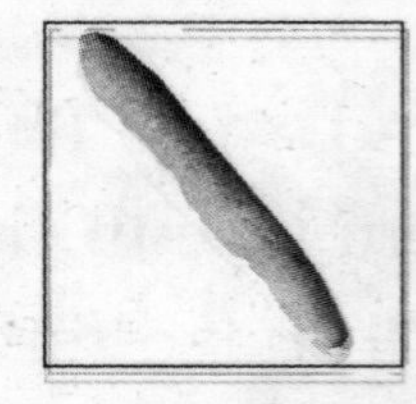  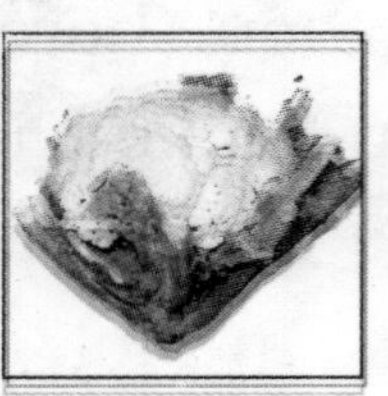 

 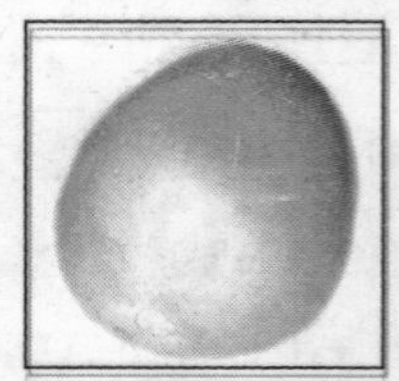   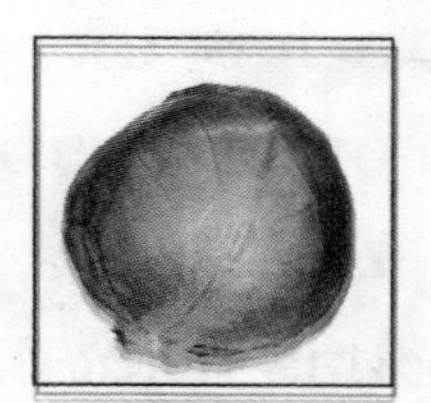

Abdul has more Questions

Nowadays Abdul keeps thinking about all kinds of plants that he sees.

Abdul saw a plant growing out of a wall in school. He wondered–

- How deep must the roots of this plant be going?
- How do the roots get water?
- How big will this plant grow?
- What will happen to the wall?
- Can you give the name of the plant in the picture?

For the teacher: The concept that roots absorb water is difficult for children (at this age) to understand. It is however important to give them opportunities to think about this relationship. Different children may be at different levels of thinking. It is important to give space to their ideas.

Have you ever seen a plant growing from a crack in a wall? Where was it? Did you have any questions when you saw it?

What were some of your questions? Ask elders and find the answers. Find out the name of the plant you saw.

Abdul saw a huge tree that had fallen on the roadside. He remembered the neem tree in his courtyard. He could see some of its broken roots. Abdul thought–

- Would someone have uprooted such a big tree or would it have fallen on its own?
- How old would this tree be?
- Abdul on seeing a tree surrounded by cemented ground, thought that how will it get rain water?

Let us talk

- Which are the oldest trees in your area? Find out from your elders how old the trees are?
- Name animals who live on this tree.
- Have you ever seen any big tree that had fallen down? What did you think when you saw it?

Unusual Roots

Have you swung from a banyan tree? What did you hold to swing? What looks like the hanging branches are actually the roots of the tree. These grow down from the branches until they reach the ground. These roots are like pillars that provide strong support to the tree. The banyan tree also has roots under the ground, just as other trees have.

There is a law against cutting trees

There was a tree growing close to a lamp post. The tree was so full of leaves that the light of the bulb was blocked. People felt that the branches of the tree needed to be trimmed. Before they do this, they need to take written permission from the government office.

Have you seen any tree which has roots growing from its branches?

Let us do this

Get together with 3-4 of your friends – From the list of things given, decide who will bring which thing.

A transparent glass tumbler or bottle with a wide mouth, rubber band or thread, some seeds of *moong*, wheat, *bajra*, mustard, *channa* (chick peas) or *rajma* (red beans) and a wad of cotton wool.

Each group will work with only one kind of seed. Soak a few seeds (5-6) overnight in a bowl full of water. Take the wad of cotton wool and wet it. Put it on the mouth of the tumbler. Tie it tight to the mouth with rubber band or thread. Remove soaked seeds from water and place them on the cotton wool. You will have to take care that the cotton wool does not dry. Observe the changes that take place for the next 10 to 12 days. Did you observe the seedlings come out of the seeds? Draw the picture of the seedling as it looks on the fourth and the eighth day.

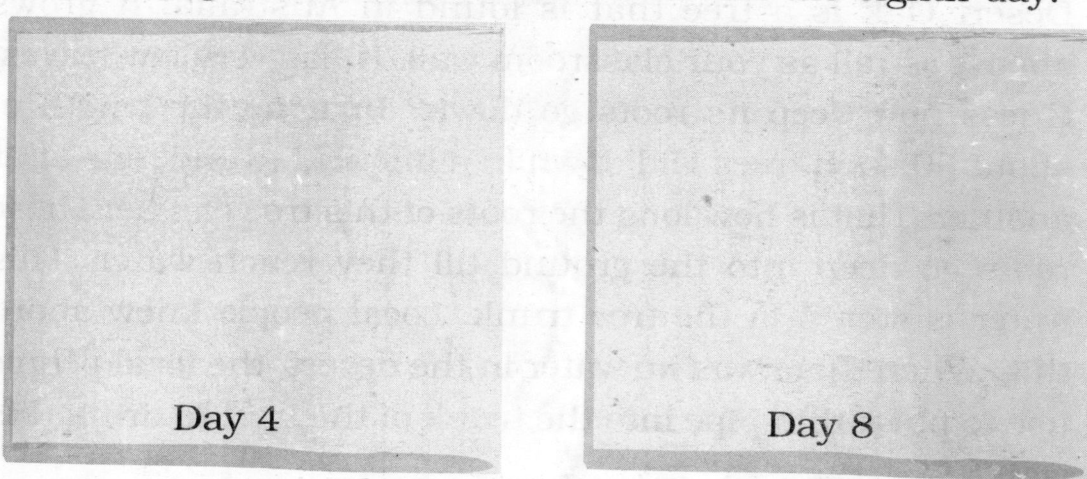

Write in your notebook

- What difference did you observe in the seeds after soaking? Compare with dry seeds and write.
- What do you think would happen if the cotton wool had been left dry?
- In which direction did the roots grow? And the stem?
- How big did the plant grow in the cotton wool?
- Did small plants come out from all the seeds?

- What is the colour of the roots?
- Did you see any hair on the roots?
- Try and pull out one little plant from the cotton wool. Were you able to pull it out? Why?
- Did you see how the roots grip the cotton wool? Do you think that the roots hold the soil in the same way? Also look at the plants grown by your friends.

Do you know?

Desert Oak is a tree that is found in Australia. It grows almost as tall as your classroom wall. It has very few leaves. Guess how deep its roots go down? Imagine the length of about 30 such trees laid down in a line end to end, one after another. That is how long the roots of this tree can be. These roots go deep into the ground till they reach water. This water is stored in the tree trunk. Local people knew about this. When there was no water in the desert, the local people use to put a thin pipe into the trunk of the tree, to drink this water.

What Grows?

Arif and Roopali did the above activity. They saw the seedlings grow. When asked – what are the things that grow? They had very different ideas about things that grow.

Arif made a list of the following – Leaves, munna, bud, puppy, nails, fish.

Roopali's list had – Moon, tree, I, hair, watermelon, mosquito, crow.

- What do you think? Which of these things listed by Arif and Roopali grow?
- Why don't you make your own list of things that grow?

Your list can include the names of things that are in Arif's and Roopali's list.

__________________ __________________

__________________ __________________

__________________ __________________

__________________ __________________

__________________ __________________

Think about yourself – in what ways have you changed over a period of time? Have you grown in any way? For example –

- Has your height increased? How much taller have you grown in the last one year?
- Imagine that you had never cut your nails! Draw a picture of your fingers in the notebook to show how they would have looked.
- What other part of your body (some people cut it regularly) keeps growing?

For the teacher: Encourage children to plant trees in the school/ colony on the World Environmental Day or any occasion. Ask them to take care of their plants.

Chapter 20
Eating Together

Class Party

The school reopened today after the vacations. The children share news about how they spent their holidays.

"When did you put *mehendi* on your palms?" Meena asked Aarti. "At my uncle's wedding," Aarti said. "You must have had a lot of fun at the wedding," David said. "Oh, yes! I enjoyed the wedding feasts the most," Aarti said. "At the wedding, we had fun with all my cousins and other relatives eating and doing everything together." Aarti said, "Why don't we do something like this in school? Let us also have some fun together." Rehana asked.

"I have an idea," David said. "Why don't we have a class party? Then we can also eat and have fun together." "We have parties in our colony whenever there is a festival. We collect money from everyone for the party. We cook some dishes and buy other things from the market," Rehana said.

Reena said, "We don't need a festival to have a party. Saturday is half-day. Why don't we plan to have our party then?"

Everyone in the class decided what each would bring for the party. On Saturday the children really enjoyed their party. There was so much variety in food. They played so many games. Everybody was so relaxed. There was singing and dancing too. They decided that they would have such a party again.

Write in your notebook

- Do you like to eat with others?
- On what occasions do you eat together with your friends?
- Have you ever had a party in your class? When? What all did you do to arrange a party?
- What did you and your classmates bring to the party?
- What all did you eat?
- Who were the people you invited for your party?
- Were there some people who work in your school, whom you could not invite? Who were these people?
- Did you wear any special dress for the party?

For the teacher: A class party is a good opportunity to get children to eat together. Children can also be encouraged to prepare songs, dances and plays for the party.

- What are the things that you can do to make the party greater fun for everyone? Discuss.

Celebrating Bihu

Bhela Ghar

Sonmoni woke up early and ran to meet her friends Tanvir, Fatima and Mazani. Today was a special day in Assam. The new rice crop had been harvested. The village was celebrating the festival of *Bihu*. The four friends sang and chatted happily as they made the *Bhela Ghar* from bamboo.

Let us read how they celebrated *Bihu*.

Sonmoni – Hurry up ! We must finish making the *Bhela Ghar* of grass and bamboo before the feast tonight.

Tanvir – Yes, today is *Uruka*. The whole village will eat together.

Fatima – Have they started preparing the feast?

Sonmoni – Yes, everyone has contributed money to buy the *bora* rice, fish and vegetables. They also arranged wood for *mezi*. Hariya and Bhadiya have not given money, but they are helping with all the work.

Fatima – What about the meat, fish and vegetables?

Sonmoni – Some people have gone to market to buy all these things. The *bora* rice has been soaked. The whole village is

For the teacher: *Magh Bihu* is celebrated on 14 and 15 of January (1st and 2nd *Magh*, the tenth month of Assamese calendar). The first day is called *Uruka*, and that day people build a temporary shed called *Bhela Ghar* and have a community feast. *Bora* is a common variety of rice used in Assam. These are 'sticky' rice. Encourage children to locate Assam on the map.

busy making *pitha*. Some people are cooking and some are roasting the sweet potatoes. Some will help to serve the food at night. In the evening, everyone will be served tea and *pitha*.

Tanvir – I am waiting to eat the *cheva* rice that we will get at the feast. I really love it.

Fatima – How will the *cheva* rice be prepared?

Sonmoni – They will light a fire and boil the water in the big *tao* (a big vessel). On this vessel, they will put the *Kadhahi* containing soaked rice and cover it with banana leaves. After some time, the *cheva* rice will be cooked and ready to eat.

Let us talk

- Where is the festival of *bihu* celebrated?
- Which are the festivals you celebrate together with other families?
- Does everyone cook and eat together on such festivals? What are some of the special dishes that are cooked? How are they cooked?
- Are some special vessels used for cooking these items? What are they?
- Which is the biggest vessel that is used? Can you draw a picture of it? Can you guess how many people can eat the food that is cooked in it at one time?

Mezi

The *Bhela Ghar* was ready. The four friends ran off to change their clothes. Soon all the people in the village got together at one place. The women were dressed in *pat* and *Muga mekhala-chador*. Sonmoni and her friends ran to the *Bhela Ghar*. The drums started to play and everyone started to sing and dance. Everyone danced till they were tired. Then they all sat down on the ground in rows and ready to eat. The food was served on banana leaves. Everyone enjoyed the feast. That night they stayed in *Bhela Ghar*.

Mazani: Sonmoni! We should go and sleep now. We have to get up early tomorrow to light the *Mezi* and *Bhela Ghar* also.

Find out and do

- Can you guess how many people must have eaten together in the village feast?
- Have you ever seen the *bihu* dance? Did you like it?
- Find out from the students in your class, the festivals that they celebrate and the special food that they eat on these days. Who cooks the special food for festivals?
- Do you wear clothes of some special colours on some festivals? Make a picture of these clothes in your notebook.
- Are there special songs that are sung at different festivals in your place? Learn some of these songs and sing them in the class.

- Learn some special festival dances. Perform these with your friends in your school assembly.
- When you meet friends of your own age do you do anything special – like play a game, chat or watch a movie? What else do you do?

Mid-day Meal

It is almost one o'clock in the afternoon. The smell of food cooking is coming from the verandah and our stomachs are rumbling. We are so hungry, we are not able to pay attention to the lesson in class.

Ding, Ding, Ding... at last, now the bell rung! All the children ran out and went to wash their hands. *Master Moshai* sent all the children to the handpump at the corner of the courtyard.

"Anondo, see that everyone washes their hands properly," he called.

After washing our hands, we all stood in queue to take our food. Some had their own boxes, and others had plates. Then we all sat down in a circle with our food. Before we started to eat, we sang together –

We play together,
we eat together.
For the good of everyone,
we will always be together.

Today there is *bhat-shukto* (rice with vegetable and gravy) in our meal. Yesterday, we had *luchi* and *chhola-dal*. Outside *Didi Moni's* room, a list of food items has been displayed. It tells what we will get every day of the week. Would it not be wonderful if on some days we got an extra treat – maybe something sweet!

There is another interesting thing about lunch time at school. Everyday we change our places in the circle and sit next to a different child. I really like this because I can meet new children and make new friends.

The food was not always very nice. Sometimes, rice was of poor quality, sometimes, it was not properly cooked. Some parents did not like their children to eat such food.

Didi Moni explained to them it was everyone's duty to make sure that the children got fresh, hot and properly cooked food. Also make sure that every child gets afternoon meal regularly. The parents also decided to help.

Now things are better. We eat fresh, hot and properly cooked food together. The younger children sometimes cannot finish all the food, but my friends and I are sometimes still a little hungry even after we eat.

Nowadays many schools give food in school during the day. It was not always like this. When my *didi* was in the primary school, children did not get afternoon meal in school. Some children come to school in the morning without eating anything. Imagine! Having to study on an empty stomach!

Find out and write in your notebook

- Write about the food given in your school. If you do not get food in school, ask a friend or someone else who gets food in school.
  - What time is the meal served?
  - What do you get in the meal at school?
  - Do you like the mid-day meal that you get?
  - Is the food that you get enough for you?

Do you bring your own plate, or do you get it in school?

- Who serves the food?
- Do your teachers eat with you?
- Is the week's menu put up on the school board?
- What will you get on Wednesday and Friday?
- If you got a chance to change the menu for the meal in your school, what would you like to change? What would you like to eat? Make your own menu.

Day	Food Items
Monday	
Wednesday	
Friday	

- If you do not get food in the school, find out why?

Mid-day Meal
EVERY CHILD'S RIGHT

Many children in our country are not able to get even one full meal every day. Many of them go to school empty stomach and cannot study properly.

Some years ago, the highest court of our country gave an important decision. All children up to elementary school should be provided with hot, cooked food. This is the right of every child.

Trring...! The doorbell rang. When Manpreet opened the door she saw Divya and Swastik there. She called out excitedly, "Gurnoor! Look who has come." Gurnoor came running. When she saw her friends she hugged them happily. "When did you come from the hostel (Boarding School)?" "Just Yesterday. Where are your parents? We want to meet them," Swastik said.

"They are at the *Gurudwara.* We were about to go there too," Gurnoor replied. "Oh good, we will also come with you," said Divya.

"You come home only in the vacations. Do you like staying in your hostel? You must be missing your parents." Gurnoor asked.

Divya said, "We do miss them, but hostel life is fun. Even if we don't always like the food, we enjoy eating together with all the children."

"You know, when someone in our hostel gets home-made food, we all rush to their rooms. That food finishes within minutes," Swastik said laughingly.

- Do you study in a boarding school? If you do not, try to talk with someone who goes to a boarding school and find out –
  - In what ways is boarding school different from other schools?
  - What kind of food do they get there?
  - Where do the children sit and eat in the boarding school?
  - Who cooks food for the children in the boarding school? Who serves the food?
  - Who washes the vessels?
  - Do the children miss home-made food sometimes?
  - Would you like to go to a boarding school? Why?

At the Gurudwara

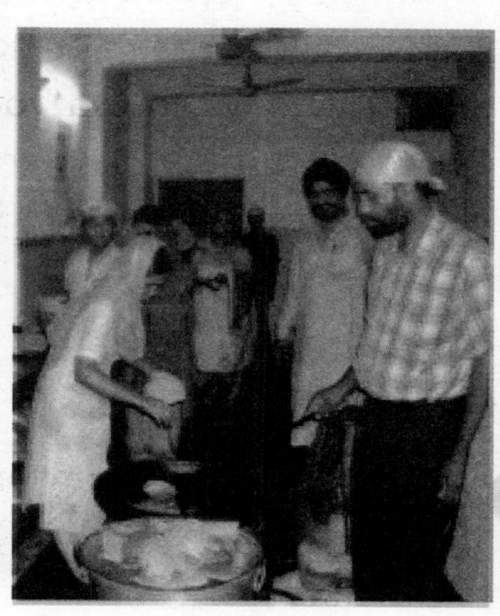

The children chatted all the way to the Gurudwara. There, they covered their heads.

They went into kitchen of the *Gurudwara*. It was very huge. A lot of activity was going on there. Food was being cooked in huge vessels. On one side the *channa* and *urad dal* was boiling.

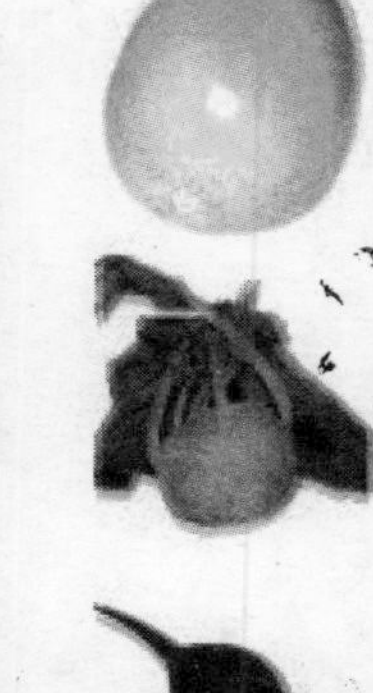

In another vessel, the cauliflower and potato vegetable was being made. "There is your Papa! Gurnoor, let us go and meet him," Swastik said.

"What are you doing here?" Manjit Singh was happy to see the children.

"Uncle, can we also help in the kitchen? What are you preparing?" Swastik asked.

Manjit Singh said, "I am preparing *kadhah prasad*. It takes a lot of effort to roast the flour in ghee in this big *kadhai*."

"This is a kind of *halwa*. Isn't it? When will you add sugar in it?" Divya asked.

They saw Manpreet's mother and rushed to meet her. Divya asked, "What are you doing Aunty?" "*Beta*, we are rolling *chapaties* to bake them in this *tandoor*." "So many *chapaties* at one go!" Divya was surprised. "Can I help?" "Sure! come and try, here everyone can help, but wash your hands first," replied Aunty.

Divya washed her hands and joined the group near the *tava*. The *tava* was very hot. She started applying *ghee* on the *chapaties* as they were being taken out of the *tava*.

Swastik wondered aloud, "Who brings all the material to cook so much food?" One of the ladies answered, "Everyone here contributes in some way or the other. Some arrange for the material, some give money, and others help in the work".

"So Swastik, how do you like it? Have you ever cooked before?" teased Manpreet.

"No, but I am enjoying working with everyone, " said Swastik. We hardly realised how all this food – *chapaties*, rice, *halwa*, *dal* and vegetable – got prepared so fast.

After *ardaas, kadhah prasad* was distributed. Some of the boys quickly laid out *durries* in the verandah and all the people sat down in rows to have *langar*. Some people served food and others served water. Everyone ate together.

After finishing food everyone picked up one's own plate, and put it in a big drum. People who were serving, ate in the end. They cleaned the place and washed the utensils.

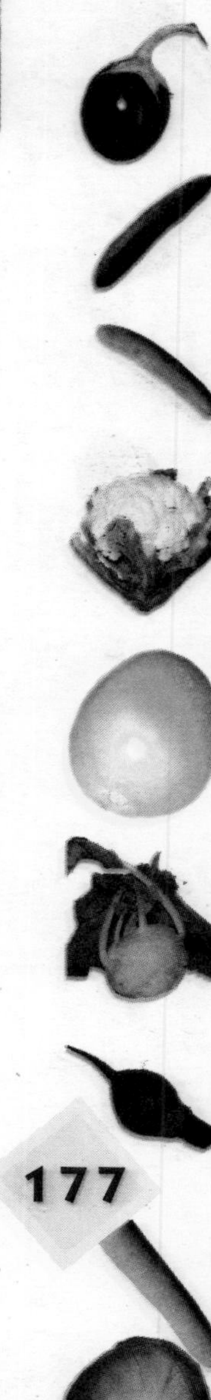

Talk about it

- The 'cooking and eating together' in a Gurudwara is called *langar*. Have you ever eaten in a *langar*? Where and when?

- How many people were cooking and how many were serving the food there?
- Are there other occasions when you have eaten with many people? Where and when? Who cooked and served the food there?

Different scenes from a Gurudwara *langar*

Chapter 22
The World in my Home

Tug of War

Once again, everybody in Marietta's family is quarrelling over watching the TV – just like they do every day! Marietta's brother wants to watch a cricket match while little Susan is eager to watch her favourite programme of song's. Mummy and Aunty are good friends but their favourite TV programmes are different. Mummy likes to watch the news while Aunty enjoys a TV serial. Marietta wants to watch cartoons and Daddy enjoys the football match. He says that he can watch TV only in the evening. Finally, everyone had to watch the football match.

Let us talk

- In your home too, do people quarrel over fans, TV, newspapers, chairs or anything else?
- In your home, who settles such quarrels?
- Talk about an interesting incident at home when there was a quarrel over such things.
- Have you ever seen people quarrelling over something elsewhere? What?

Why the Difference?

It is 7 o'clock in the evening. Pratibha is hurrying home from her friend's house. Her brothers Sandeep and Sanjay are busy playing round the corner with their friends. They are in no hurry to go home. Even if they are late, nobody will scold them.

Pratibha thinks that this is not fair. Why should there be one rule for her and another for her brothers? But what can she do?

Let us talk

- Does this kind of thing happen in your house or in any of your friend's house? What do you think about this?
- Do you think that there should be different rules for girls and boys, women and men?

◎ Think – what would happen if girls had to follow rules made for boys and boys had to follow rules made for girls.

Pilloo Aunty

One day, Pilloo Aunty took Phali and Nazu and their friends to the beach. What a good time they had! They played in sand and water, and then went for a ride on the Giant wheel. After that they ate *bhelpuri* and bought balloons. Then everybody enjoyed some icy cold *kulfi*. When the *kulfi*-seller asked for money, he made a mistake. He charged for five *kulfis* instead of seven. The children thought, "Hurrah! We have saved money." But Pilloo Aunty paid the money for seven *kulfis* to the *kulfi*-seller.

The children will always remember what Pilloo Aunty did that day.

◎ If you were to write a different ending for this story, how will you end it?

- Is there anyone in your family who is like Pilloo Aunty? Who?
- What would the children have thought if Pilloo Aunty had paid less money to the *kulfi*-seller? What do you think about this?

What Should I Do?

Akshay loves his grandmother very much. She loves him dearly too. She talks to him about many interesting things. Anil is Akshay's friend. His grandmother likes Anil too, but one thing that she tells Akshay again and again is that he should never eat or drink anything at Anil's house – not even a glass of water! "They are very different from our family," she says.

One day there was a volleyball match in the big ground near Anil's house. It was a hot day and everybody was tired and thirsty after the match. Anil invited everybody home. Anil's mother gave water to all of them, and they drank it. When Anil handed Akshay a glass of water, he suddenly remembered his grandmother's warning. Akshay stared at Anil, not knowing what to do.

Talk about it

- What do you think Akshay will do?
- Why was Akshay confused?
- Why do you think Akshay's grandmother warned him not to drink even water in Anil's house?
- Do you know of anybody who thinks like Akshay's grandmother?
- Do you agree with Akshay's grandmother?
- What do you think Akshay should do?

Who will Decide?

Dhondu comes from a very large family. His elder uncle looks after the family – their fields, money matters, etc. He decides about all the small and big things for the family.

Dhondu has always worked in the fields. But now, he wants to do something different. He would like to borrow some money from a bank and buy a *chakki* machine to grind grain. There is no such machine in their village. Dhondu is confident that this new work will help him earn more money for his family. Father has agreed to let him try the new work. But his elder uncle is not agreeing to this.

For the teacher: These examples reflect some situations that we face in our daily life. These often affect us in different ways. Encourage children to think about these and to express how they feel about them.

Talk about it

- If you were in Dhondu's place what would you do?
- Has it ever happened with you that you wanted to do something but the elders in the family did not allow you?
- Who takes important decisions in your family? What do you feel about this?
- How would you like if only one person made all the decisions for your family?

I Don't Like It!

Meena and Ritu were going home after playing hopscotch. "Come on, come to my house," pleaded Meena, pulling Ritu by the hand.

"Is your Uncle at home? If he is, I will not come," Ritu answered.

"But why do you say that? Uncle likes you. He was saying – bring your friend Ritu home and I will give both of you lots of chocolate."

Ritu pulled her hand away from Meena saying, "I am scared of your Uncle. I do not like it when he even touches my hand."

Saying this, Ritu went home.

For the teacher: Some children may have similar experiences as Ritu did. It will help to build their confidence and feeling of support, if children can discuss this in class. In case you feel the need, you could talk individually with some of the children. If there is a counsellor in the school, you could take their help.

Talk about it

- Have you ever disliked anybody's touch? Whose touch did you dislike?
- If you were in Ritu's place, what would you do?
- What else can be done when such things happen? Discuss.
- Everybody's touch is not the same. Ritu did not like it when Meena's uncle held her hand, but she liked to hold Meena's hand. Why do you think there was this difference?

Chapter 23
Pochampalli

Vani and Prasad live in a village called Mukhtapur. Their home is always filled with bundles of bright coloured threads. Their mother and father and everyone else in the family, are weavers. The weaving that they do is very beautiful and special.

Mukhtapur village is in the Pochampalli town of Andhra Pradesh. Most of the families in this town are weavers. That is why the special cloth that they weave is called Pochampalli.

The villagers have been doing this work since a long time. Vani and Prasad's parents learnt weaving from their elders.

For the teacher: Make the children aware that most traditional arts are learnt at home. There are many different handicrafts to be learnt like Pochampalli. You could discuss other traditional occupations like carpet weaving, toy making, *Itr* production, etc.

Process of making pochampalli sarees

Now Vani and Prasad also help their parents after coming back from school. This weaving requires hard work, and many different things have to be done before actually weaving.

From thread to Cloth

Father brings bundles of thread from Pochampalli town. Mother then puts these threads in boiling water to wash away the dirt and stains. Then everybody works to dye the thread with bright colours. These threads are then dried and rolled into bundles. These bundles are put onto looms and the cloth is woven. Silk cloth and silk sarees are woven from the silk thread. Cotton thread is used to weave cotton sarees, cloth, sheets, etc.

The loom has many needles. The size and number of the needles changes according to the design. The weavers weave the beautiful Pochampalli sarees in bright colours. Through their traditional craft they have made their region world famous.

A Craft in Danger

Great skill is needed to weave such special sarees. It also takes many days of hard labour. After all this, it is difficult to get a good price for these sarees. Silk is becoming expensive day-by-day. Big shopkeepers give very little money for the sarees, though they themselves sell them at very high price. That is why many weavers are giving up their family craft. Many are leaving their villages to work as labourers in big cities. We need to solve this problem by helping them get a better price. Otherwise, this precious craft will be lost forever.

For the teacher: In many traditional occupations, different kind of tools and skills are used. Emphasise that the entire family participates in making one thing, and that everybody has different responsibilities and duties.

Discuss

Vani and Prasad learnt this beautiful craft from their family members. When they grow up, do you think they will be able to teach their children the skills of this craft?

Write in your notebook

- Have you ever seen anybody weave something on a loom? What were they weaving and where?
- The threads of a saree are dyed. Do you know of any other thing that is dyed?
- If you visit Vani's village it seems as if the entire village is weaving sarees. Do you know of any other work which many people living in one place do?
- Do they make some article?
- Find out the process of making the article? What are the different steps?
- Do men and women do different kinds of work to make this article?
- Do children also contribute in making this article?

Find out and write

- Talk to an ironsmith, a carpenter and a potter about the nature of their work.

____

____

- Where did they learn to do their work?

____

- What else did they need to learn to be able to do this work?

- Have they taught this work to anybody in their family, or to anyone else?

- The table below has a list of different kinds of work that people do. Do you know people who do such work? Write their names in the first column. In the next column write from whom have they learnt their work?

Kind of work	Name of people you know who do this work	Where did they learn this work from?
Cloth weaving	*Prasad and Vani's parents*	*From their elders*
Cooking		
Cycle repair		
Flying aeroplanes		
Sewing and embroidery		
Singing		
Making shoes		
Flying kites		
Farming		
Cutting hair		

For the teacher: There are many places like Pochampalli in India that are famous for making special things. These things have become famous by the name of the place where they are made, like – Kullu shawls, Madhubani paintings, Assam silk, Kashmiri embroidery, etc. Do you know any more examples? Discuss this in the class.

Today, there was a lot of activity at Maalu's house. *Chittappan* and his family were coming home after five years. *Chittappan* had got a job in a country called Abu Dhabi five years ago. Since then he had lived there. Maalu and her *Appa* went to the airport to receive them.

After the plane landed, the passengers had to wait for some time to collect their luggage. At last *Chittappan, Kunjamma* and their two children could be seen coming out. "How big Shanta and Sashi have grown," *Appa* said.

Soon the many suitcases and bags were fitted into the taxi and everyone was on the way to Maalu's house.

"Shanta, you must be very tired after your long journey, *Appa* told me that Abu Dhabi is another country, far from India," said Maalu.

For the teacher: *Chittappan* – Father's younger brother in *Malayalam*. *Kunjamma* – Father's younger brother's wife in *Malayalam*.

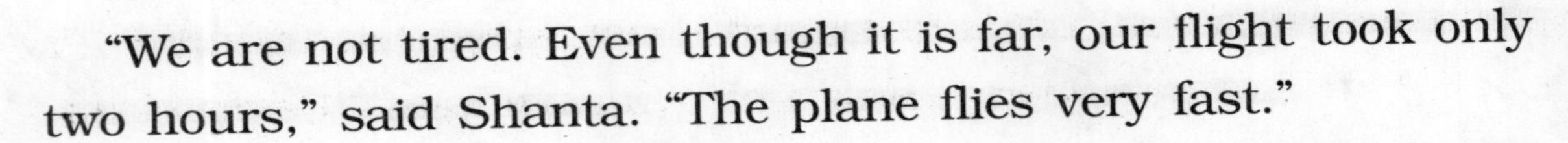

"We are not tired. Even though it is far, our flight took only two hours," said Shanta. "The plane flies very fast."

Maalu was surprised. She remembered that when she had gone on a school trip to Chennai, they had spent almost 12 hours in the train. And on the map, Kochi and Chennai seemed quite near. Maalu, Shanta and Sashi chatted all the way home from the airport. Maalu remembered how much fun she had on her school trips. She wanted Shanta to tell them all about her trip from Abu Dhabi.

Dust All Around!

"Did you see many interesting things from the plane?" asked Maalu.

"Most of the time we saw only clouds because the plane was flying so high, even higher than the clouds," said Shanta. "But before it went so high, we could see that we were flying over sandy areas. It was sand but the colour of the sand kept changing – white, brown, yellow, red, black. We saw mountains made only of sand." "They are called sand dunes," added Sashi.

"I have seen sand only at the seashore," said Maalu.

"Then you should come to visit us," said *Chittappan*.

"The countries around Abu Dhabi are located in a desert area. Even if one drives a little away from the city, one can see miles and miles of sand – no trees, no greenery – just sand."

"I used to dream of the thick greenery and cool water around our home in Kerala," said *Kunjamma*. "I am so happy to see all this after such a long time."

"The children have almost forgotten how it feels when it rains. You know it almost never rains in desert areas," said *Chittappan*. "Water is really very precious over there. No rain, no rivers, no lakes, no ponds. Even below the ground there is no water." "But," added Sashi, "there is a lot of oil under the sandy soil. So petrol is easily available in these countries." "In fact petrol is cheaper than water," said *Chittappan*.

By this time the taxi had reached Maalu's house. Shanta and Sashi were surprised to see so many fruit trees–coconuts, bananas, jackfruit, papaya, betelnut ... so many kind of trees! Sashi said, "We used to see only one kind of tree there – the date palms – because it is the only one that can grow in the desert. The date is the most common fruit."

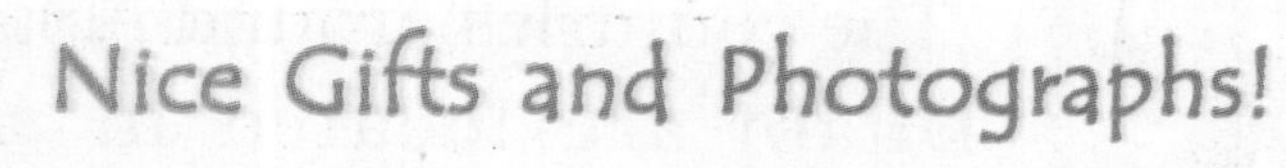

Nice Gifts and Photographs!

After they had met everyone, *Kunjamma* unpacked their bags. They had brought gifts for everyone. They gave dates for everyone to eat. The dates were very sweet and tasty. Sashi showed Maalu some notes and coins. Shanta explained that the money they used in Abu Dhabi was different and was called *Dirham*. It had some writings in their local language – Arabic. They also showed many photographs of the place where they lived.

Chitappan gave Maalu a globe. He said, "Maalu, why don't you locate Abu Dhabi on this? Locate Kerala also." The children enjoyed playing with the globe and looking for different places on the globe. Maalu found Chennai and Kochi also.

In the evening everyone sat in the verandah, enjoying the breeze and looking at the photographs. They saw that in Abu Dhabi the buildings were tall with many storeys and big glass windows. Maalu said, "You must be getting nice cool breeze through the big windows." *Chittappan* said, "We cannot open the windows because of the heat. It is air-conditioned inside

where everyone stays. As the weather is very hot, people wear loose cotton clothes and keep themselves fully covered – even the head is covered. This protects them from the strong sun."

Maalu enjoyed looking at the pictures and finding out about the other country from her cousins. She constantly kept comparing her city with the things that they described about Abu Dhabi. She decided that she would make a project report about Abu Dhabi for her class.

Discuss and write

- You can also make a small report comparing Abu Dhabi with the place where you live. You can use some of these points mentioned below while writing the report. You can also draw pictures or put photographs.
  - The climate and weather
  - What people wear
  - The trees and plants
  - The kind of buildings
  - The traffic on the roads (kinds of vehicles)
  - The common food items
  - The language
- Why do you think many trees cannot grow in desert areas?

  ___

- Do you have any relatives who live in another country?

  ___

- How long have they lived there? Did they go there for studies or for work? Was there any other reason?

- Look at these currency notes

Write the value of each note in the box near its picture.

- To which country does this currency belong? How did you know?

____

- Whose picture can you see on the notes?

____

- Can you find any number on the notes (other than the value)?

____

- Do you think that two notes can have the same number?

____

- Take a ten rupee note and observe it carefully. How many languages can you see on the note?

____

- Write the name of the bank given on the note.

____

Match the coins

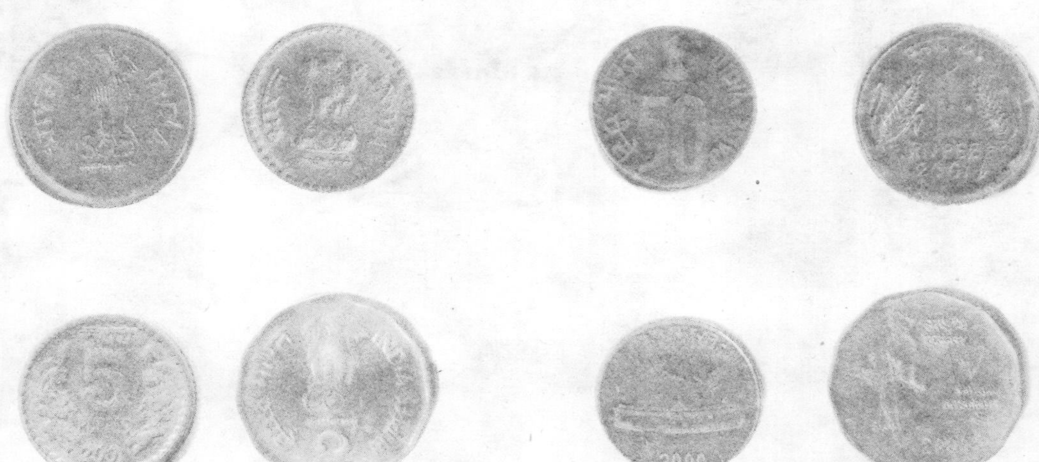

- How many of these coins do you recognise?

____

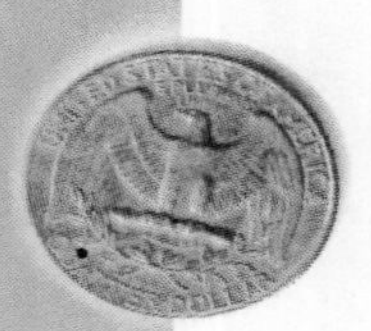

- What is written on each coin other than the value.

- Look at these notes. Do they all belong to India? Put a circle around notes that are not Indian. Find out which country do they belong to.

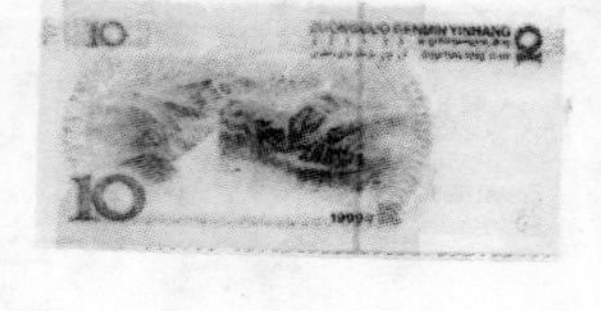

Chapter 25
Spicy Riddles

I can be powdered fine
To make food hot and spicy,
If too much of me is added
I make you gasp – shheee... shheee...
Your eyes and nose begin to water
And you cry!
Think and tell me who am I?
Tell me quickly, who am I?

Grind me and powder me –
To make your food look yellow,
I am mixed in oil by granny
And applied to wounds quickly,
I heal all wounds – big and small,
That is why I am loved by all!
Think and tell me who am I?
Tell me quickly, who am I?

Small and round like a pearl,
I am black when I am whole.
I can be powdered coarse or fine
A sharp and spicy taste is mine,
Whether it is salty or sweet
I am added as a special treat,
Think and tell me who am I?
Tell me quickly, who am I?

I am a small and skinny chap
Sometimes I am brown and
sometime black,
Added to hot oil and ghee
I spread my fragrance all around me,
When I am roasted.
Curd and jaljeera are favourite to me.
Think and tell me who am I?
Tell me quickly, who am I?

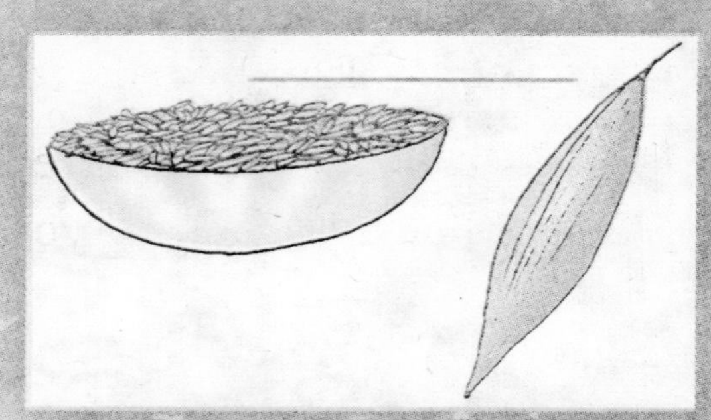

I look like Zeera though green am I,
To make your stomach
healthy I always try,
Eat me always after your meal
I refresh your mouth, you
surely feel,
Think and tell me who am I?
Tell me quickly, who am I?

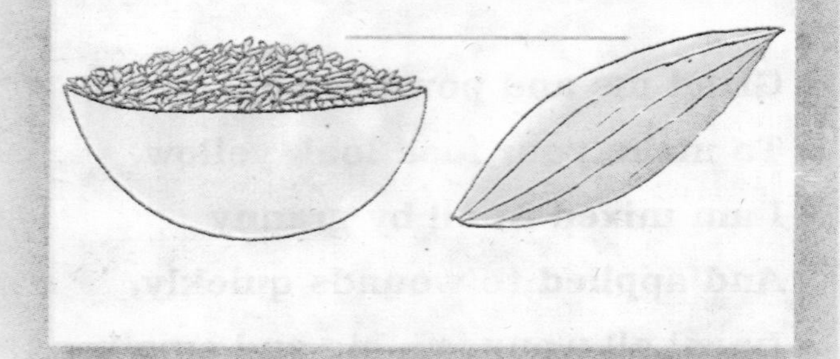

I look like a nail but a bud am I,
Chocolate brown colour and a
strong smell have I.
When your toothache
makes you shout,
I soothe the pain in your mouth.
Think and tell me who am I?
Tell me quickly, who am I?

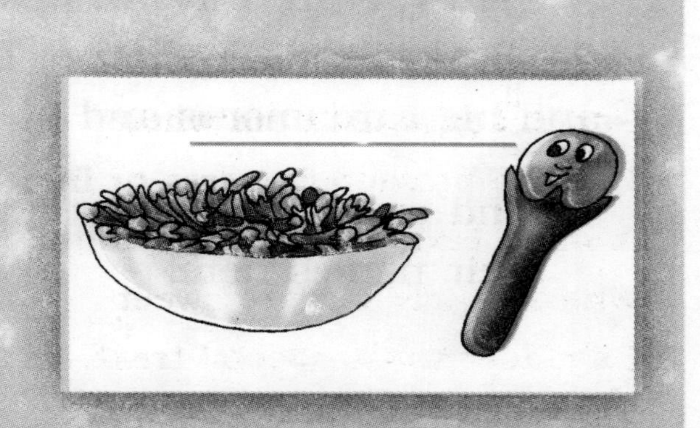

Now try and make your own riddles about two other spices. Ask those riddles in your class. Draw pictures of the two spices in your notebook and write their names.

- Find out which spices are used in your house for cooking. Make a list and look at your friends' lists too.

_____________ _____________
_____________ _____________
_____________ _____________

- When your grandparents were young, which spices were used most in their kitchens? Find out from them and write here.

____
____

- Name one spice which is put into both sweet and salty things.

____

- Find out what is put into food to make it taste sour.

____

I am Kuttan. I live in Kerala. There is a garden of spices in the backyard of my house. There I see plants of *tejpatta*, small and big cardamoms and black pepper grow.

- Find out whether any spices are grown in your area. Write their names here.

____

- Bring some whole spices to class. Write their names in the table. Close your eyes and try to recognise each spice by smelling and touching each one in turn. Put a (✓) mark in front of the ones you recognise. If you do not recognise any, put a (×) mark.

No.	Smell	Touch	Name of the spice
1.			
2.			
3.			
4.			
5.			

Let us try making a spicy potato *chaat*!

- For this you need –

  Boiled potatoes, enough for everybody in the class.

  Salt, red chilly powder, mango powder (*Amchur*) or lemon, according to taste.

For the teacher: *Garam Masala* : A powder of a mixture of several spices like – cardamom (small and big), clove, cumin seeds *(zeera)* cinnamon.

- Roasted cumin seeds (*zeera*), black salt, and garam masala, if it is possible.
- Fresh coriander leaves.

Peel the boiled potatoes and cut them into small pieces. Now add salt, red chilly powder, mango powder or lemon juice according to taste. To make your *chaat* more delicious, add a little roasted cumin seeds, black salt and coriander powder. A pinch of *garam masala* can also be added at the end. Mix the potatoes well. Sprinkle chopped coriander leaves on top and hurrah! Your spicy *chaat* is ready to eat!

- Did you enjoy the potato *chaat?*
- Just imagine, if there were no spices to make the potato *chaat*, how would it taste?
- Try to learn and make a different kind of *chaat* and enjoy it with all your friends in class.
- How do spice-less and very spicy things feel on your tongue?

Chapter 26
Defence Officer: Wahida

Have you ever seen her photograph anywhere? She is Lieutenant Commander Wahida Prism, doctor in the Indian Navy. She is one of the few women who has worked on a naval ship. She is the first woman to lead a parade. This is considered to be a very big honour in the armed forces.

We specially spoke to Wahida for this book. Let us read what we spoke.

Question – Wahida, tell us something about your childhood and school.

Wahida – I come from a very small village called Thannamandi. This is in Rajouri district of Jammu and Kashmir. I did my schooling from a government school. Most of the girls from the village studied in my school. However, few of them ever thought of what they would do

For the teacher: Encourage children to locate Jammu and Kashmir on the map of India.

after finishing school. I always wanted to become someone special and move forward in life. I was very interested in higher studies and wanted to complete the tenth class. In my area, it was a new thing at that time. My mother and father had to face many problems because of this. We even had to move out of our village. We then went to live with my grandmother in Rajouri. I did my twelfth class from there.

Question – So you always thought differently right from the beginning?

Wahida – Even when I was very young I wanted to do something different. I was very fond of riding a motor-cycle. We are three sisters. My father wanted one of us to become a doctor and one a teacher. He wanted the third daughter to become a lawyer or join the police force. I have become a doctor in the Indian Navy and my sister is in the Jammu Police Force.

Question – How did you become a doctor?

Wahida – I worked very hard. My friends and family members helped me a lot. I got admission in Jammu Medical College. I studied for five years and did my M.B.B.S.

Question – How did you get into the Defence Forces? Didn't your family stop you?

Wahida – Oh, no! They felt that a job in the Forces would be the best thing for me. When I was very small, I would see army officers in our village. I wanted to be like them. This was really a very big dream for me! While in school, I attended camps,

For the teacher: Children can be informed about all the three forces. For this, help can be taken from children from the defence background.

climbed mountains and was a 'Girl Guide'. After I became a doctor, I appeared for an interview to join the Armed Forces. I got selected there and received a training for six months.

Question – Why did you join the Indian Navy? Do you not have to live on the naval ship?

Wahida – Well, I am very fond of travelling. I like to see different places. I wanted to go to far-off places. I was born in the hills and now I am working in sea. I really enjoy it.

Very few lady-officers have worked on a ship. I am one of them. Earlier, women were not allowed to go on Naval ships. When an opportunity was given, I myself went forward and gave my name. I even want to go in a submarine. I want to do everything which people think women cannot do. At present women are not allowed to go in submarines, but whenever it is allowed, I will certainly go.

Question – So what happened to your degree of M.B.B.S?

Wahida – I am a doctor, but in Indian Navy a naval doctor does not just give medicine to patients. She is in fact, a medical officer. The ship goes to sea for three-four months at a time. There, it is my responsibility to make sure that everybody on the ship stays fit and healthy. I carry out medical check-ups of all the officers and sailors. I also have to make sure that no

For the teacher: Let this discussion inspire the children to dream about doing big things, and to work hard towards fulfilling their dreams.

garbage collects and there are no rats on the ship. Rats and garbage can spread diseases. I must keep everybody, ready for any medical emergency on the ship. In case there is an accident on the ship, (like a fire), everybody must be ready to deal with it.

Question – Is there a hospital on the ship?

Wahida – 'First aid' is given on every naval ship. Each ship has one doctor and two or three assistants. Necessary medicines and some equipment are also available. All these things are kept in a small room.

Question – You are the first woman to lead a passing out parade. You must have worked very hard for this.

Wahida – My seniors gave this opportunity to me after seeing my performance for three years. I felt happy that they had chosen me and showed faith in me. So I practiced very sincerely.

Question – Tell us something about that parade.

Wahida – In a parade, four platoons march behind the leader. Thirty-six commands have to be given during the entire parade. These must be given in a very loud voice so that it is heard till the rear. The voice should also reach the spectators sitting on the other side of the ground.

For the teacher: Other occupations may also be discussed while teaching this lesson.

Question – Didn't you feel nervous leading four platoons?

Wahida – I was not nervous, but one has to shout thirty-six commands. If you forget even one, the entire parade can get spoiled. I practised every morning and evening for a month. But, I have been participating in parades since school.

Question – What is the meaning of the word 'Prism' in your name?

Wahida – My father gave this name to me. A prism is a kind of glass which reflects seven colours. My father wanted me to be like a prism and that is why he started calling me by this name from my childhood itself.

- Do you know anyone who is in defence services? Is the person in the Navy, Army or Air Force?

  ____

- What work do they do in the force?

  ____

- Would you like to join the defence services?

  ____

- Which of the three would you like to join – the Army, the Navy or the Air Force?

  ____

For the teacher: Lay emphasis on the fact that women are now joining the defence forces and police in great numbers. Show children a prism in the class.

- In which other jobs do people wear uniforms as in defence services?

____

- Wahida works as a doctor in the Indian Navy. Can you name five other occupations in the Navy?

____

____

- Have you ever seen a parade? Hold a parade in your own school and try giving thirty-six-commands – for example, "Parade, Eyes Right", "Don't move", "Close in", "Open file". Can you add some more commands to this list?

______________ ______________ ______________

- Talk to a doctor and find out about her/his work.

____

____

- Do you know any woman who has done something unusual? Talk to her in the same way as we talked to Lt. Cdr. Wahida Prism. Think of the questions that you will ask. Find out why she has chosen that work. What were the difficulties she faced in her life?

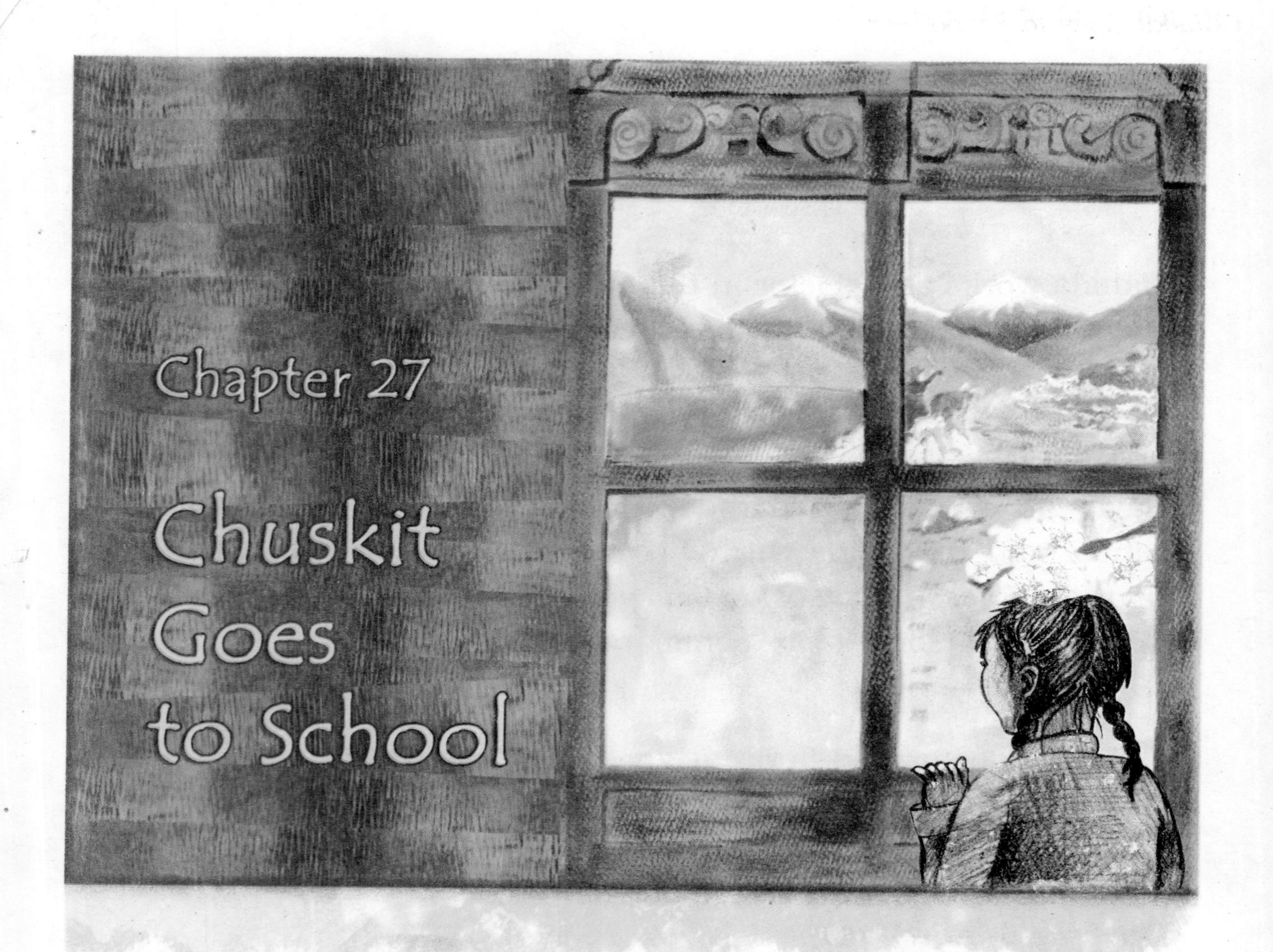

Chuskit's Dream

Today is a special day for Chuskit. It is so special that last night Chuskit could not even sleep. Do you know why? Chuskit is ten years old, but today she is going to school for the first time. She has been waiting for this day since long.

Chuskit's school is not very far from her house. You have to take the big road and then walk along the lake. Cross the river near the poplar trees, and then after a small climb, you reach the school. This is how all the children of Skitpo Pul village reach their school. All the children, but not Chuskit.

Chuskit amongst photographs from Ladakh

- How do you go to school?
- Find out where Ladakh is. What kind of a place is it?

At first Chuskit did not know that she was different from other children. But slowly she found that she could not do the things that other children could. It was because of her legs. Since birth, Chuskit could not use her legs.

Chuskit's Chair

All day, Chuskit used to sit near the window and draw pictures. Her mother (*Aama-le*) said that Chuskit made the best drawings. This made Chuskit happy. But Chuskit was happier when one day her father (*Aaba-le*) got a chair which had wheels. She quickly learnt how to sit in the chair and how to move it – back and forth. Chuskit was so happy because now she did not need her father to carry her everywhere. When she wanted to go out she would tell her mother to put her in the wheel chair. Now, she could come outside on her own.

Chuskit would see the other children every morning. They would be laughing and playing on their way to school. She wished that she could also go with them.

One day Abdul came to her house with a letter. When he saw Chuskit, he asked her why she did not go to school. Chuskit told him sadly, "I can not walk. *Aaba-le* cannot carry me all the way to school everyday. I cannot even wheel my chair as the road to school is not level. Also, how can I cross the river?"

Abdul asked, "But would you want to go to school if you could?" Chuskit was excited. She said, "Of course I want to go to school just like all of you. I want to study and play... ."

Her *Meme-le* (grandfather) stopped her and said, "Chuskit do not dream. You know that this is not possible."

- What are the things that you enjoy doing in school?

  ____

- Do you like going to school?

  ____

- Would you like it if you never could go to school?

  ____

A Good Idea

Abdul went back from Chuskit's house, but he had started thinking of how to get Chuskit to school. He explained about Chuskit to the Headmaster and talked to the teachers till they agreed with his thoughts. Now everyone got together to work so that Chuskit's problem could be solved. They made a plan so that Chuskit could bring her wheel-chair by road to school.

For this, the uneven road had to be made level. One group of children started to level the road. Another group worked to level the area near the river. But there was still a problem. How would Chuskit cross the river? The older children took help from the teacher to make a small bridge with wood across the river. Everyone happily worked hard. They wanted Chuskit to come to school.

Chuskit's *Aama-le* and *Aaba-le* gave hot tea and biscuits to everyone. Chuskit's *Meme-le* had tears in his eyes – not because he was sad, but because he was very happy!

By the evening, the work was done. All the children were happy. But the happiest of all was Chuskit. Her dream was about to come true.

And today, it was that special day. Chuskit was all ready. She was eager to go to school!

Talk about it

- Who all helped Chuskit to reach school?
- If you were Abdul what would you have done?
- At last, Chuskit could reach school. Do you think that she may face some difficulties in school? What kind of difficulties? If you were Chuskit's friend, how would you help her?
- Do you have ramps in your school on which a wheelchair can move?
- Do you know any child near your house who cannot go to school because of some difficulty? Would you like to help such a child? How will you help?
- Look at the buildings around your house. Can a wheelchair go inside the building?

Let us do

- Draw pictures of a ramp and a wheelchair in your notebook.
- Why not make your own bridge? For this, use material that you can find around you – Ice cream sticks, plastic spoons, small sticks, rope, string etc. Your friends can also make bridge.
- In a group of friends make a model showing fields, rivers, mountains, roads, and railway tracks, etc. You can use clay, sand, pebbles, twigs, leaves. Place your bridges at different positions on this model.

Chuskit and her School

Help Chuskit to reach school